BEFORE
THE LAST
RESORT

BEFORE
THE LAST
RESORT

3 SIMPLE QUESTIONS
TO RESCUE YOUR MARRIAGE

GEORGE KENWORTHY

FamilyLife Publishing®
Little Rock, Arkansas

Before The Last Resort: 3 Simple Questions To Rescue Your Marriage
FamilyLife Publishing®
5800 Ranch Drive
Little Rock, Arkansas 72223

1-800-FL-TODAY • FamilyLife.com

FLTI, d/b/a FamilyLife®, is a ministry of Cru®

Unless otherwise indicated, Scripture quotations are taken from the Holy Bible, New International Version®. Copyright © 1973, 1978, 1984 International Bible Society. Used by permission of Zondervan Bible Publishers.

Scripture quotations marked NASB are taken from the NEW AMERICAN STANDARD BIBLE®, Copyright © 1960, 1962, 1963, 1968, 1971, 1973, 1975, 1977, 1995 by The Lockman Foundation. Used by permission. (www.Lockman.org)

Scripture quotations marked NLT are taken from the Holy Bible, New Living Translation, copyright 1996, 2004. Used by permission of Tyndale House Publishers, Inc., Wheaton, Illinois 60189. All rights reserved.

Scripture quotations marked AMP are taken from Amplified® Bible, Copyright © 1954, 1958, 1962, 1964, 1965, 1987 by The Lockman Foundation. Used by permission. (www.Lockman.org)

Scripture marked ESV are taken from The Holy Bible, English Standard Version®, copyright © 2001 by Crossway Bibles, a division of Good News Publishers. Used by permission. All rights reserved.

ISBN: 978-1-60200-721-5

© 2005, 2014 by George Kenworthy

FamilyLife® and FamilyLife Publishing® are registered trademarks of FLTI.

Design: Kent Jensen · Knail, LLC

Printed in the United States of America

21 20 19 18 17   1 2 3 4 5

FAMILYLIFE®

"I am the LORD, the God of all mankind.
Is anything too hard for me?"

JEREMIAH 32:27

CONTENTS

INTRODUCTION   1

CHAPTER 1   YOU GOTTA HAVE HOPE   5

CHAPTER 2   WHEN PRAYER DOESN'T WORK   21

CHAPTER 3   ATTITUDE IS EVERYTHING   41

CHAPTER 4   LOOK WHO'S TALKING   55

CHAPTER 5   HAVE YOURSELF A GOOD, CLEAN FIGHT   71

CHAPTER 6   BLUEPRINT FOR A MARRIAGE MAKEOVER   87

CHAPTER 7   ROMANCE BY THE BOOK   113

CHAPTER 8   SEEING IS BELIEVING   127

APPENDIX A   THE COMMUNICATION DATE   143

APPENDIX B   FAMILY BACKGROUND DISCUSSION SHEET   147

APPENDIX C   PRAYING SCRIPTURE TO SAVE YOUR MARRIAGE 151

HELP-ME-HELP-MY-FRIEND GUIDE   161

ACKNOWLEDGMENTS   193

NOTES   195

INTRODUCTION

I have a hunch.

My guess is that a close friend, your pastor, or a family member gave you this book. If so, let's be honest. You probably forced a smile and, for a quick second, contemplated using it as fire starter the moment this well-meaning person walked away. I don't blame you. After all, if the "For Sale" sign is planted in the front yard and your lawyer is telling you that you've got to get custody of the kids, you must be wondering: What's this book going to tell me about saving my marriage that I haven't already tried?

If you are a woman, I imagine you've been processing the troubling issues in your marriage for months—if not years. You've been to counselors and yet you remain frustrated that the guy you married is so unbelievably "dense," which is why you've probably been planning your exit strategy for weeks.

You're so done rearranging deck chairs on the Titanic.

Besides, who has time to read, right?

Especially if you're worried about where you'll be living after the house is sold.

You've got kids to juggle, a spouse who may be uncommunicative or hostile, and a job where you're not allowed to bring in your problems. You're sleeping less at night primarily because you're exhausted from walking on eggshells all day. What you long for isn't another "marriage saving" book. My guess is that you want to find the quickest way to stop the pain, and some shortcut to lead you out of the maze of bitterness, disillusionment, and hurt.

I don't blame you if you have those feelings.

When you were first married, all you wanted was to love someone special and experience love in return. Now, however, a root canal seems more appealing than spending another day trapped in a difficult marriage. I understand that your heart is capable of withstanding only so many bruises and that even now you may be clutching on to your last ounce of dignity.

Frankly, I wouldn't be the least bit surprised to hear you say that, after many months of useless therapy, you've resolved yourself to the inevitable: a divorce. While you're numb at the thought of calling it quits—not to mention struggling with the pressure, embarrassment, and guilt over your decision—what other choice do you have? You're exhausted from trying to pull your marriage out of the quicksand.

On the other hand, maybe you're a guy who's finally awakening to the fact that something isn't right between you and your spouse. Like an early morning fog that's lifting, you're seeing more clearly what your wife has been trying to get you to see for years. Or, perhaps she moved out in the middle of the night and left you with a note that caught you completely off guard. Now, much like finding yourself on a runaway train, you think all you can do is assume the "crash position" and hope for the best.

Whether you're a man or woman, it's also possible that you've been caught in an affair and can't imagine turning back to make things right. You might claim that you don't love your spouse anymore and you're convinced your marriage is over. Your choices demonstrate you mentally checked out long ago. And, you've probably announced that you never loved your partner to begin with.

No matter what your circumstances are, I am convinced that if you stay with me until the end of this short book, a genuine miracle awaits you.

How can I be so confident?

Simply put, for the last thirty years I've witnessed countless miracles firsthand. You see, I pastored a church in Minneapolis where we saw God heal about 90 percent of the marriages of all the couples we counseled.

You might want to read that again.

I'm talking about healing marriages with deep, hard-core problems. Couples ensnared in a thick web of deceit, adultery, physical or verbal abuse—even homosexual or lesbian entanglements. Time and time again, I've stepped back in amazement as I've watched God radically transform the ashes of a failed marriage into a thing of beauty.

This is why I am convinced beyond a shadow of a doubt that He desires to do the same for you. Even if your marriage isn't in desperate straights, I believe you'll still find our conversation in the pages ahead beneficial for your marriage or that of a friend who may be struggling.

In this book, I will show you how you can experience healing, renewed hope, and a revival in your marriage. But don't take just my word for it. Throughout these pages I'll share with you dozens of powerful stories from those whose marriages were over and who now—sometimes three, five, even fifteen years later—are happier, healthier, and closer than they ever dreamed possible.

Now, if I have learned anything from three decades of working with couples in your situation, it's that few have the emotional capacity or time to work through a long list of exercises or homework assignments. This is why, at the end of each chapter, I'll provide you with the "One Thing"—a simple, yet practical application that will help you move toward healing. These powerful tips and tools will enable you to reconnect with your spouse while the Lord is supernaturally working behind the scenes to restore your marriage.

Don't get me wrong. There are no quick fixes, silver bullets, or magic wands to wave. I'm a realist. At times you will experience a barrage of doubt or a flood of anger. At other times you may feel as if you're treading water, barely able to keep your head above the crashing waves of despair.

Let me assure you that you are not alone.

In fact, Jeremiah, one of the writers of the Bible, has already thrown you the ultimate lifeline with his observation, "Sovereign LORD, you have made the heavens and the earth by your great power and outstretched arm. Nothing is too hard for you" (Jeremiah 32:17). Nothing means *not one thing*—including restoring a stagnant, dying marriage. Indeed, the Creator who made heaven and earth longs to rescue you from the deep waters you find yourself in today.

I realize you may have already given up hope. But, I challenge you to dare to hope again as you and I begin an adventure to discover what can happen when we say yes to the power of Jesus. That is the heart of this book. The God that chose you, who loves you and sent His Son, Jesus, to die for you, is a God who has resources in heaven—riches, strength, power, and might—that are beyond your imagination.

Based on my many years of involvement with hundreds of couples, as well as what God has revealed in the Bible, I am convinced that God cares about you personally. He cares about your family, your marriage, and He especially cares about the fact that you are hurting today.

Will you give Him one more chance?

I can think of no better story to set the stage for your personal road to a relationship revival than the story of John and Amy.[1] If you're ready to discover what God can do and what He desires to do for your marriage, read on.

CHAPTER 1

YOU GOTTA HAVE HOPE

The first time I met John and Amy for counseling, Amy announced that she had already been to two Christian counselors and both had advised her to file for a divorce. I suppose the reason for this assessment was that Amy claimed she didn't love John anymore. In fact, Amy made it painfully clear that she was in love with someone else, and as far as she was concerned, it was time to move on.

Since John and Amy had been attending the church where I was pastoring, they decided to see me before they called it quits. You might say this was a last resort to salvage things between them. After listening to them vent, I asked them a series of questions, which, frankly, may appear simplistic at first glance. As you'll see in a moment, I am convinced that the way a couple responds to these three questions is fundamental to their future success together.

Here's what I asked them:

1. DO YOU BELIEVE THAT THERE IS A GOD?
2. ARE YOU WILLING TO APPLY THE PRINCIPLES OF THE BIBLE TO YOUR LIFE?
3. WILL YOU PRAY FOR GOD TO STRENGTHEN YOU AND YOUR SPOUSE?

Both John and Amy acknowledged that they believed in God. Both agreed to apply the principles of the Bible to their life. And, both said they would pray for God to touch them and their marriage. So far, so good. I proceeded to tell them, "On the authority of God's Holy Word, the Bible, and the power of His promises, I will absolutely guarantee that this marriage will come back together!"

Then, like pouring cold water on the spark of hope in John's eyes, Amy informed us that she was unwilling to give up her relationship with her lover. The thought of leaving someone who had become her soul partner was too much to ask.

Amy maintained that her lover understood her . . . he knew how to meet her needs . . . he cared for her in ways that John never did . . . she loved him with all of her heart. And since she no longer loved John, how could she turn her back on her lover? Amy knew that God did not approve of her adulterous relationship—and neither did I. But I also knew that there was nothing I could do to convince her to abandon her boyfriend.

God could.

I was prepared to wait for God to convict her and give her the strength to do what was right. From my experience, such conviction could come quickly, or it might take a number of months. After all, if Jesus could raise his dear friend, Lazarus, from the dead, He could convict Amy of the dead end that pursuing this man represented.

In the meantime, I provided them with a number of tips and tools I use in my marriage counseling: I showed them how to do a communication date and how to handle conflict biblically. We talked about sex and examined their family backgrounds. We explored how they could show love for each other. We also closed our sessions with prayer and my reminder that when God touched their marriage, we would all know it.

Then we waited.

After about nine months of counseling, I recommended that they take a trip to Florida. The other man was still very much a part of Amy's life, and I thought the time away from him, as well as two weeks alone with her husband, might help rekindle their marriage. Guess what? It didn't.

When they got back to Indianapolis, a defiant Amy called and fumed, "My time with John in Florida was awful. I have had it. I am canceling our counseling appointment for tomorrow. I have contacted my lawyer and have filed for divorce."

About thirty minutes later John called echoing Amy's opinion. He said, "George, our time in Florida was an absolute disaster. Amy is still in love with our neighbor. We're wasting our time thinking there is any hope for us. I have contacted my lawyer and filed for a divorce."

My heart sank with the bad news. It was obvious that my best efforts had accomplished nothing. Worse yet, John and Amy both believed in God but were feeling more weak and more hopeless than they had ever felt before.

But God was not finished.

About an hour after her first call, Amy called again. This time I immediately perceived something was different in her voice. "I just got back from driving around the city," she said. "While I was out, I saw a billboard that had this simple message, 473-PRAY. When I got home, I turned on the TV and I saw the same billboard with the same message. I dialed the number and spoke with a prayer counselor for about fifteen minutes."

Not wanting to interrupt her, I held my breath.

"George, I can't explain it, but I believe God has spoken to me. I think He wants me to end my relationship with my boyfriend and work on my marriage with John. What do you think?"

"Amy," I said, thrilled at the breakthrough, "this is what we have been praying for over the last nine months. You have just heard the voice of God. Until now you have heard words from me and from others about God, but now you have heard from God Himself. This is wonderful! How can I help?"

She said, "I need to tell my boyfriend what has happened today." In fact, she felt an urgency to confront her boyfriend that evening and wanted me there for moral support. I assured her I wouldn't miss it.

Amy and I met about ten minutes before her boyfriend arrived. We prayed together and I encouraged her with several verses from the Bible. Moments later, this man, who had been at the center of the conflict in her marriage, arrived. They met in a warm embrace in the middle of the room. He whispered, "I love you."

"I love you, too," she said.

Then, obviously puzzled by my presence in the room, he asked, "So, what's going on?"

Amy answered, "I have heard the voice of God today. God told me that I need to break off my relationship with you and really work on my marriage to John. I will be moving out of the apartment this week. I think I need to move back in with John."

"Amy, I don't understand. You just said you loved me."

"I do," she said, taking a step back. "But I have to do what God has told me."

Stunned, he shot her a bewildered look. "If that's what you want, Amy, then fine. I'll leave."

With that, he left. I am convinced that this fellow never understood what she was saying. Perhaps he thought that when Amy got back together with John, she would come to her senses and realize how awful her marriage had been.

That never happened. Why?

Because Amy had heard from God! We still had more work to do in a counseling setting, but at least now there was hope. With the distraction of her lover out of the picture, it seemed like just a matter of days before Amy felt a fresh love for John begin to bud. Gradually, John learned how to meet her needs. Both learned how to express love in ways that communicated love to each other. It was a miracle of marital healing.

That was about fifteen years ago.

Not long ago Amy stopped by to see me. She was carrying her newest addition to their family. With an infant nestled in her arms and a wide smile on her face, Amy positively glowed. She couldn't wait to let me know how happy she was, how well they were doing, and how thankful she was to the Lord for what He had done.

I said, "Amy, I have been telling folks for years about what God did for you. I call you the Billboard Lady. What do you tell your friends about what happened?"

Her face lit up: "It was a miracle!"

John and Amy's story is evidence of what God can do for your marriage. I am convinced that you and I desperately need to hear more powerful stories like theirs. These living examples remind us that God still saves marriages. That, my friend, is what this book is about. No matter what your situation, I'm confident that there is hope for any marriage—as long as you are willing to believe that God, through His Spirit and the wisdom found in the Bible, can radically change your lives.

OPEN TO A MIRACLE

You may be thinking, *George, I'm open to a miracle, but my situation is different. John and Amy were both willing to pray that God would intervene in their marriage. But does God still work when your spouse won't agree to pray with you for a breakthrough?* That's a valid concern. Guess what? I have found that as long as there is one partner who is willing to trust God to heal the marriage and who will seek help, miracles happen. Let me give you two brief examples.

First, take Mark and Missy, a couple who attended our church. Mark had had an affair but confessed his wrong behavior and expressed a sincere desire to make his marriage work. For her part, Missy was so hurt by his betrayal, she lost all hope that their marriage would survive. Rather than come to our office, Missy decided to go to the Twin Cities and see a counselor who advised her to seek a divorce from Mark.

Meanwhile, each week in church Mark filled out a prayer request card asking for the staff to pray for his marriage. Aware that Mark and Missy were struggling, I invited Mark to come in for counseling. He did—alone. Keep in mind his wife had become convinced that a divorce was their only solution. So, for several weeks I worked with Mark on what he needed to do to deepen his faith in God and helped him discover how to show love to his wife.

Missy knew about Mark's efforts to change but insisted she would not put the brakes on her decision regarding a divorce.

Finally, I asked a member of our counseling team to meet with Missy. This lay counselor had watched God work a miracle after infidelity had almost torn her own marriage apart. Missy reluctantly agreed to meet with her and to listen to what the Lord had done in her life. God used that meeting to persuade Missy that maybe there was a thread of hope for their marriage after all.

Several weeks later, Missy agreed to meet with Mark and me. During our first session she insisted that she still had little hope for their reconciliation, but the next week she came back again. Missy cautiously continued to work on their relationship. Over time they committed to having regular communication dates and they developed a conflict resolution "contract." However, the real breakthrough occurred when Missy decided to pray with us at the close of a session.

I'm a strong believer in asking both husband and wife to pray aloud when we close our time together. Soon after Missy agreed to pray with us, God touched their marriage in a dramatic way. What was once a "lost cause" became a miraculous story of restoration, one that they readily share with friends and our church to this day.

Second, consider Grant and Penny.

This couple was very active in our church in Denver. Both sang in the church choir and taught elementary-aged children in our Sunday school. However, Penny suffered from bipolar disorder and, unfortunately, was not on medication. As a result, she lost interest in outside activities. She had regular bouts of depression and went through each day with about as much energy as a houseplant.

Grant, by contrast, was a hyperactive businessman—a high-stakes player who pushed himself as a top achiever in his field. While not exactly an adrenaline junkie, he enjoyed a range of sports. Their chances of finding common ground were as likely as finding rain in the desert.

As you might expect, Grant became disappointed with a spouse who frequently was not interested in his company.

By the way, it is not uncommon for a couple to drift apart in their interests, hobbies, and activities the longer they are married. One key to a successful long-term marriage is to find those areas of common ground where both partners can stay connected on a daily basis. Some wash dishes by hand the old-fashioned way because that gives them time to talk and accomplish a simple task. Others make a point of taking an after-dinner walk each night.

Evidently, Grant and Penny didn't maintain even basic levels of interaction. Not surprisingly, the distance and the seeds of temptation grew in Grant's heart. While Grant maintains he never intended to have an affair, a woman he met on a business trip was everything he hoped Penny would be: outgoing, vibrant, professional; someone with whom he could talk business, someone who laughed and enjoyed life. He was drawn to her vivaciousness and quickly developed an intense friendship. In a moment of weakness, they shared a bed. While Grant knew that what he had done was wrong, he attributed his infidelity to his wife.

He blamed Penny saying that the only reason he was drawn to this woman was that he had needs—personal, social, conversational, and sexual—that Penny wasn't fulfilling, so he found fulfillment elsewhere. Grant was defiant over his affair because, after all, "it was Penny's fault." After an initial conversation with Penny, Grant refused to talk further about what he had done. He wouldn't speak with Penny about it and he certainly was not willing to talk to anyone in the church about the affair.

Frustrated, Penny came to us for help by herself. Grant's infidelity naturally intensified her depression. We provided Penny tools to help her overcome her melancholy mood. Over a period of time, God gave her victory, and the darkness that once surrounded her began to lift.

Grant couldn't help but notice the change in his wife and eventually agreed to join us for marriage counseling. He had broken off the relationship with the other woman, so we focused on his and Penny's future. Grant was a bit testy at first, but as he and Penny asked God to heal their marriage and as they completed their assignments, God restored their relationship. What's more, Penny became one of the women I trained to do lay counseling with our team.

Think about it. If you are feeling suffocated by the weight of your circumstances, consider Penny's transformation. Here was a woman who felt like she was losing her mind and, in fact, did lose her husband to an affair for a season. Yet now, she and Grant give hope to numerous couples who are struggling with their marriage.

Let me ask you something. In spite of how you may view your current circumstances, is it possible that the Lord might one day use your testimony to help reconcile others who are struggling?

STILL CHANGES LIVES

Let me be clear. In each of the stories I've shared, I don't want to give you the impression that there's a secret formula at work. In case you missed it, the golden thread tying these wonderful tapestries together is threefold:

- AN ACKNOWLEDGMENT THAT THERE IS A GOD
- A WILLINGNESS TO TRUST WHAT HE HAS SAID IN THE BIBLE AND FOLLOW HIS INSTRUCTION
- THE COMMITMENT TO PRAY FOR GOD TO HEAL THE MARRIAGE

If that approach sounds just a tad simplistic or naïve, frankly, there was a time when I might have agreed. But let's step back and think about what's going on here. When boiled down to the basics, one issue remains: How big is your God? If you and I trust God for our eternal destiny—in other words, if we believe Jesus has the power to save us from hell when we die—can we not also trust Him for a few lesser things here on this earth?

That question pushed me to the brink of a crisis of faith at one time. You see, I love the Bible, and I love to teach it to people who want to apply it to their lives. However, I discovered early in my ministry that many of those who came to church would listen to me declare the wonderful and dramatic way God had changed lives throughout history on Sunday morning. But when Monday rolled around, these same folks claimed that their marriage was the exception to what I had taught.

Talk about disheartening.

As a young pastor in my late twenties, I didn't know what to do when these couples came into my office and told me that they didn't love each other anymore. They knew that God hated divorce, but they were also under the impression that God didn't want them to suffer in a marriage that made them miserable. Some told me that they had prayed for their marriage and had tried for years to make things work, but they had no hope.

I wanted to tell them that if they just trusted Jesus, He would heal their marriages. But that seemed to be too simplistic; besides, I knew realistically that they probably had heard similar advice before. At one time, maybe they believed Jesus could save their marriage, but too many emotional scars and too much pain had robbed them of any vestige of hope.

Looking back at the couples I counseled then, typically one spouse had committed adultery. Usually, at least one would say that love for the partner wasn't there anymore, and often would go as far as to say that love had never been there in the first place. Some even said that they believed the only way to get back into God's will was to get a divorce.

If there was no love and if there had been an affair, what hope was there? I kept asking myself that question at the same time I was preaching on Sunday, "With God all things are possible!" (Matthew 19:26). Can you imagine the conflict in my soul? Eventually, I came to the point where I found myself asking God, "Are the truths I preach on Sunday meaningful at all for those with hurting marriages? Are You and Your promises in the Bible powerful enough to provide hope and healing when all hope is gone?"

In my heart, based upon what I knew from my study of God and the Bible, I knew the answer to those questions was yes. But practically speaking, I was at a loss as to how I might help the hopeless regain hope. Then the answer hit me. I wouldn't say I heard the audible voice of God, but His message was unmistakable, "George, you preach from the Bible. Do you believe it?"

I said, "Lord, you know I believe what You have said in the Bible is true."

God said, "Good, tell folks who are hurting to follow what I say."

This crisis of faith occurred while I was in the process of taking courses toward a PhD in religion at the University of Iowa. In my program I had taken several courses in counseling. I also took several psychology courses as I completed MDiv and ThM degrees at Trinity International University. I was tempted to find solutions for these troubling marital problems in psychology, but for the more intense marital problems, my background in psychology was not the answer.

What I now know is that God wanted me to see that He alone is the answer! I thought I had always believed He was the answer. What transformed me was a moment I had with God when He told me to dare people to believe His promises in the Bible and to trust Him for what they needed. Ultimately, that led me to start asking those three key questions of every couple that I counseled.

Ever since I started to embrace the beauty and simplicity of this approach, I have witnessed repeated evidence that an affair isn't enough to keep God from working. The conviction that love is gone cannot stop the power of God to change lives. Even the certainty that there is someone else whose love is purer and better than our spouse's will not thwart the work of God—if we will say yes to all three questions.

As I said previously, from that time more than 90 percent of the couples I've worked with have rebuilt their marriages and their love for each other after acknowledging that God exists, applying the principles found in the Bible, and praying for God to strengthen their marriage. They now enjoy a fullness, a closeness, and a friendship with their spouse that they never thought was possible.

You might be wondering, "But what about the 10 percent who don't find healing for their relationships? Why doesn't this approach work all of the time?" Good question. Let me set the stage by sharing with you the heartbreaking story of Alex.

A FORK IN THE ROAD

Alex was a highly successful executive in the food industry. He enjoyed the finer things in life, not the least of which was a home worth more than three-quarters of a million dollars in a highly sought-after suburb. He wasn't the flashy type. In fact, everybody who met Alex found him to be a likable and engaging person. I was introduced to him because he was having difficulty in his marriage.

As we began to dig into his situation, it became apparent that Alex was having an affair—with a younger man. Since his boyfriend didn't have money, you might say Alex was kind of keeping this guy. Alex and I would have regular conversations about what Jesus would think of this arrangement. Without skipping a beat he'd say, "Given my background in the church, Jesus would think this was wrong."

Alex was not ignorant of what the Bible said on the subject. Nor, to his credit, did he attempt to twist the Bible to accommodate his behavior. On more than one occasion I'd ask, "What do you think Jesus would have you do?" Without hesitation, he'd say, "I think Jesus would have me break off the relationship."

With my encouragement, Alex got involved with Sex Addicts Anonymous and began attending regular meetings. Several weeks later, he confessed that on the way home from the meetings he'd sometimes drive into his old cruising neighborhoods. On more than one occasion when he was either going to or coming from his SAA meetings, he would fall into temptation because he was thinking about the part of his life that he would be denying.

This went on for several months. Every time I was with Alex, he would mention how great it was to talk to me because he felt condemned wherever he went. Evidently, he sensed the love and compassion of Jesus, so he continued to return to my office. Don't get me wrong. I wasn't sugar coating what the Bible taught about his choices. I constantly asked him, "What do you think Jesus would have you do?" He clearly knew the right path, but invariably he couldn't bring himself to do what Jesus would have him do.

Keep in mind, throughout this ordeal his wife was involved in our women's activities at church. Both were active attendees of the church, too. They came together every Sunday and loved hearing the weekly teachings from the Bible. One problem. He was struggling between holding on to this young guy and preserving his marriage. Finally, we reached a point where I felt the Lord prompting me to pin him down to make a decision on what to do with his life.

I asked him, "Alex, what are the implications if you don't get back together with your wife?"

He thought a moment. "Well, George, if I don't choose my wife, I know I'll be rejecting Jesus. I know I'll be rejecting my Christian friends, I know I'll be turning my back on God, and I know I'll probably get AIDS and die. And on the other hand, if I choose my wife, then it's the good life of a follower of Christ, the wholeness that I'll have, it's even eternal life. I know that. I realize that eternity could even weigh in the balance."

Here's the tragedy: That day Alex left my office and chose death. This is an example of a marriage that didn't work out. Why? It boils down to a decision: *obedience or disobedience.* Alex failed to obey what he knew to be true. Here was a guy who said that he wanted what God wanted, but refused to do what God would have him do—even given the choice between life and death, cursing and blessing. Alex consciously chose cursing and had to live with the results of that.

As you'll see in a moment, our need for obedience (which leads to God's blessing) is actually found in a book from the Bible named after Micah, a prophet from biblical times. In other words, you and I have to be willing to stop engaging in destructive behaviors once they are pointed out—or there can be no chance of growth or healing in our marriages.

TRUST AND OBEY

Micah had been given a message from God because the people in Micah's day were "theologically orthodox," which is to say that they believed in God and in His teachings. However, there was little evidence of God at work in their lives because they failed to put His instruction into practice. At the time of Micah's writing, the people of Israel, also known as the children of God, were a hopeless, powerless people. What was even sadder was that they didn't know any better.

Evidently they thought they were living the way that God intended them to live—even though they were not obeying Him. Micah challenged them with these words: "Is the Spirit of the LORD impatient? Are these His doings? Do not My words do good to the one walking uprightly?" (Micah 2:7 NASB). Don't miss what's going on here. The Lord has personally promised you and me that He is patient and will "do good" for those who obey—who are "walking uprightly."

Talk about good news!

That's where obedience comes into the picture. Go back to the story of Alex. He knew what he should have done according to God's instruction in the Bible. He enjoyed coming to church, too. However, Alex didn't follow through with obedience. Jesus rightly asks, "Why do you call me, 'Lord, Lord,' and do not do what I say?" (Luke 6:46). Indeed, how could we expect Alex's marriage to succeed?

Like Alex, we say we believe in God and in the promises of the Bible, but too often there is little evidence of the power of God in our lives because we don't follow through in obedience to His instruction. So, when a marriage becomes desperately hopeless, we can't imagine doing anything but calling it quits. We, like the people of Israel in Micah's day, just don't get it.

God wants to give you a hope and a wonderful future. As the Lord said through the prophet Jeremiah, "Obey me, and I will be your God and you will be my people. Walk in all the ways I command you, *that it may go well with you*" (Jeremiah 7:23, emphasis added). What an awesome promise!

Are His promises difficult to believe?

If so, consider what He has done for John and Amy, Mark and Missy, and Grant and Penny. Each of these couples is proof that God does heal hurting marriages. Your name could be on that list, too. There can be hope for any marriage as long as you are willing to believe that God, through His unlimited power, can radically change your life.

That said, how would you answer these three questions?

1. DO YOU BELIEVE THAT THERE IS A GOD?
2. ARE YOU WILLING TO APPLY THE PRINCIPLES FOUND IN THE BIBLE TO YOUR MARRIAGE?
3. WILL YOU PRAY FOR GOD TO STRENGTHEN YOU AND YOUR SPOUSE?

If you are ready to cling to the promises made by the Creator Himself, if you are ready to trust and follow His guidance, and if you are hungry to discover what God can do for you and your spouse, I've got good news. The tips and tools that I use to help couples discover God's best for their families are right here in this book.

These tools are totally transferable and are based on what is taught in the Bible—thoroughly biblical. And they work! What's more, you don't have to be a trained counselor to use them. The first tool is learning how to utilize the gifts God offers you to steer your marriage toward healing. I'm excited to explore those truths with you in chapter 2.

THE ONE THING

Using a 3" x 5" card or sticky notepad, write out this Bible passage from the book of Jeremiah and then place it on your bathroom mirror: "I am the LORD, the God of all mankind. Is anything too hard for me?" (Jeremiah 32:27). Use it as a daily reminder about the power of God to change your marriage.

CHAPTER 2

WHEN PRAYER DOESN'T WORK

For three years, my accountability partner and I met every Saturday morning—I'll call him Mike. Each week we held each other accountable to behavioral goals we had set for ourselves. From our personal Bible study, prayer, and family life to our respective jobs, all of our goals were quantifiable, specific, and measurable. During those three years there was nobody that I knew better than Mike. We played and prayed together. Our families even vacationed together. I was a pastor and Mike was a top businessman for a nationally known company.

Mike clearly understood my world because for several years he, too, had been a pastor of a growing church in California. This former preacher, teacher, counselor, and man of God was my best friend. I called on him frequently to preach for me when I was out of town.

Mike was more than an adequate guest preacher. My congregation eagerly bought recordings of his messages and always looked forward to his preaching. You can imagine my shock during one of our Saturday mornings together when Mike announced, "I don't love Jan anymore. I love my boys, but I don't want to be married to their mother."

As a pastor, Mike had regularly heard members of his congregation say something like that to him. He knew all the right "Christian" answers. He knew exactly what the Bible said about divorce and marriage. And, according to his own position, he knew what he was contemplating violated the teaching of the Bible.

When I pressed him for an explanation, he said, "George, I am tired of doing the right thing! All my life I have done what is right. I just don't have the strength to do it anymore."

Mike was a great father and had been a good husband. There was no other woman in his life. He had, in fact, conscientiously resisted advances from several women. But, for whatever reason, Mike's feelings for Jan were gone. In his mind, his marriage was broken and he could not figure out how to put the pieces back together again.

Worse, he didn't even want to try.

One Saturday as we talked, his eyes filled with a mixture of sadness and near desperation. Through his tears he said, "George, what's wrong with me? I know God is a great and awesome God. I know He says, 'I hate divorce!' (Malachi 2:16). I am afraid that if I do what I want to do, He will judge me. I fully expect His judgment, but I still don't want to be married. I cannot make myself love Jan."

What could I say to my friend?

There wasn't any verse in the Bible that I could show him that he didn't already know as well as I did. He could easily parrot the pious platitudes. He had preached on promises such as, "God works for the good of those who love him" (Romans 8:28) and "If God is for us, who can be against us?" (Romans 8:31). For a long moment I found myself at a complete impasse. That is, until I felt the Lord pinpointing in my spirit exactly what Mike needed.

Mike lacked power.

Too much of his Christian life had been about duty. He knew Christ personally. He had experienced God at work in his ministry, but somehow at this critical juncture there was no power for his marriage and, understandably, he was tired of trying to patch things up on his own.

I said to Mike, "I believe you need God to give you the power for your marriage that you lack! This is not about human effort and energy. I believe you are engaged in a spiritual battle, and what you need are the spiritual resources only God can give."

Maybe you can relate to what Mike was experiencing. Perhaps you've been a Christian for many years. You might have been involved in the church or led a small group in your home that studied the Bible. You may have even volunteered as a Sunday school teacher or donated your time and resources in an outreach to youth.

Whatever your situation, I believe many people who struggle in their marriages today are like my friend, Mike—tapped out. They've been busy doing the things Christians do and have become trapped in a cycle of duty. They either lack or are unaware of the three gifts God makes available to all believers: His hope, riches, and power. Without these three gifts, we're easily left hopeless, weak, and defeated in our marriages.

How do we receive these gifts? The answer is found in a letter written by the apostle Paul to the Ephesian church.

HOW TO UNLEASH THE POWER OF PRAYER

When our marriages are in trouble or when our families are falling apart, our prayers tend to be preoccupied with a long list of concerns for our spouse and our children. While that seems understandable, I find it interesting that Paul, who dearly loved the Ephesian church and who was grieved by their many weaknesses, didn't focus his prayers on their troubles, which included everything from sexual immorality, stealing, and greed to marital mistreatment. Rather, he focused on God and on His son Jesus.

What should we pray when our marriages are weak? We should pray as Paul did in Ephesians 1:15–23 and 3:16–22. Read these passages now, and be encouraged.

It's as if Paul is saying that before you can address your marriage, your children, or your job, you must focus on your relationship with God. The main reason your attention must be on God is that the fight you are waging in your marriage "is not against flesh and blood, but against the rulers, against the authorities, against the powers of this dark world and against the spiritual forces of evil in the heavenly realms" (Ephesians 6:12). In other words, there's a supernatural dimension to this tug of war you're feeling with your spouse.

Make no mistake about this: Satan has painted a bull's-eye on your marriage. The last thing he wants is for your union to succeed. Why? The devil, also known as the father of lies, knows that your marriage is actually a picture of Christ's union with the church—His bride. You see, the Bible teaches that one day there will be a beautiful wedding in heaven between the church (that's all Christians), who will become the bride, and Jesus, who is the Bridegroom.

If Satan can sabotage your relationship, he gets to tarnish the picture of Christ as the Bridegroom loving us, His bride. Whenever a marriage fails, the devil is pleased because that breakdown sows the seeds of brokenness into the next generation. And speaking of the impact on children, Satan knows that a healthy Christian marriage and home is the best place to raise the next generation of children who will grow up to love God. That's why he's literally hell-bent on sabotaging all marriages, including yours and mine.

Is it any wonder marriage can be such a challenge?

So, according to Paul, where should we start when we find ourselves in a hurting marriage that has left us hopeless, weak, and defeated? We focus on God, that's number one. And, of course, we do this through prayer. But Paul makes it clear that what and how we pray is critically important.

Here's a perfect example.

In his book *How to Win Over Depression*, best-selling author Tim LaHaye reports on a survey conducted by a pastor who was working with a group of Christians struggling with depression. This pastor divided them into three groups: Group A was provided with techniques to improve their mental well-being, Group B was given proper instruction in prayer and actually spent time praying together, and Group C was simply told to figure out how to pray on their own at home. Watch what happened. LaHaye writes:

> After several weeks almost 50 percent of those who were counseled had improved. Of those who prayed together on a weekly basis under the guidance of a biblically-oriented instructor, 85 percent were helped. But of those who prayed privately without instruction not one improved, and several showed deterioration.[2]

Why was there such a drastic difference between those in Group C and those in the other groups? LaHaye explains, "Upon investigation it was discovered that every uninstructed person had indulged in the sin of self-pity in his prayer life."[3]

You see, if we don't know what and how to pray, our prayers are ineffective and can actually hurt us. We tend to focus on our needs rather than on the help God offers us to meet our needs. What, then, should we pray when our marriages are weak? We should start by praying for the gifts the Father offers us (Ephesians 1:15–23). God desires for us to get to know Him more intimately. And in the context of that relationship, He will provide the resources to overcome discouragement and despair.

The first gift presupposes that we do not know everything there is to know about God. That concept should not be hard to grasp, but when we are in pain, it's too easy to assume we know everything we need to know about God. That was the fundamental problem of a wealthy man in the Bible named Job.

GOD OF THE GALAXIES

Job knew a thing or two about pain.

Remember the story of Job? Here was a distinguished man who had everything—wealth, stature, servants, and ten beautiful children. You might say that Job had a charmed life. One day, all that Job owned—including his children—was swept away as a test of his faith. Unbeknown to him, Job's personal drama was played out before the watchful eyes of a heavenly audience.

Job and his three friends, Eliphaz, Bildad, and Zophar, wrongly assumed that the only possible explanation for his suffering was that

God was punishing him for his sin or for disobedience on his part. On three separate occasions, Job's bad assumption about the character of God led him to actually accuse God of being his enemy (see Job 13:24; 19:11; 33:10).

God rightly thunders back at Job, "Who is this that darkens my counsel with words without knowledge? . . . Where were you when I laid the earth's foundation? Tell me, if you understand" (Job 38:2, 4). God gets at the heart of Job's problem when He asks, "Would you discredit my justice? Would you condemn me to justify yourself?" (Job 40:8). Imagine the irony of this scene. Here's the God of the universe being questioned and accused by Job.

Before we bash Job for his shortsightedness, far too often you and I make the same mistake when swirling in the midst of our misery. With the undertow of pain dragging us further out into the sea of doubt, we underestimate the greatness of God. We reduce His capacity to save our marriages to a level that our puny minds can understand. In the end, we belittle the only One who has the power and strength to rescue us from the mess we've made of our relationships.

Job ultimately repents saying, "You asked, 'Who is this that obscures my counsel without knowledge?' Surely I spoke of things I did not understand, things too wonderful for me to know" (Job 42:3). Job comes to admit that he complained and acted wrongly because he did not really understand who God is. Job needed (and got!) a revelation of the character and person of God.

Perhaps the perfect place for us to begin is to confess that we simply have a dwarfed view of God and need to know Him more deeply. That, surprisingly, is something that Moses, a leader of the Israelites, yearned for on a regular basis—I say surprisingly because Moses, as you may recall, was the human instrument that God used to perform the miracles of the ten plagues in the land of Egypt and the parting of the Red Sea. And on Mount Sinai, Moses received the Ten Commandments from the hand of God. Throughout his life Moses talked to God like no human ever had.

Yet, after all of those unmatched encounters with God, Moses hungered to go deeper. He wasn't content to rely on past experiences with the Lord. His sole desire was to learn everything he could about this amazing Savior. Moses prayed, "If you are pleased with me, teach me your ways so I may know you and continue to find favor with you" (Exodus 33:13). In light of Moses' example, consider this: What might happen to you and your marriage if you prayed to receive a fresh perspective of God?

Don't sprint by that question too quickly.

You see, like Job wallowing in the midst of his pain, our tendency is to accept a partial truth about the character of God that, in turn, produces despair and disappointment in our relationships. On the other hand, when we come face-to-face with Jesus, when we spend time in His company, and when we allow our understanding of God to be stretched, we cannot help but be changed. In Moses' case his face literally glowed!

In other words, your view of God is critical to your view of His ability to make over your marriage.

Big God = Small problems.

Small God = Big problems.

What else might we have confused regarding God's character and His love for us when we are hurting?

CHARACTER OF GOD

There seems to be two primary inadequate views of God that quickly get us into trouble. First, I have spoken to many who emphasize the justice of God to a fault. They see God as a hard-nosed judge with a holy scowl perpetually ensconced on His face. There's no tenderness. No leniency. No empathy. Almost looking for a way to drop the hammer on us. Case in point.

Some time ago I visited with Vanessa who was very depressed. She was thoroughly miserable in her marriage and in life. When I asked why her outlook was so bleak, she said, "I hear you regularly talk about having a personal relationship with Christ. I have prayed to ask Jesus into my heart several times, and it does not seem to make any difference. I don't feel like Jesus is in my life."

When I asked Vanessa to explain what made her feel as if Jesus was not in her life, she said, "I don't see how Jesus could be pleased with me because I am not able to pray the way I should or read the Bible as much as I should. I feel so guilty, I get depressed when I think about my faith."

As I listened, I sensed that Vanessa might have a wrong assessment of God's character. I prompted her to describe her view of God. Vanessa said, "Well, God is holy. He is just. He is almighty. He is pure. He is perfect." She's right, as far as her list went. But there's another side to God she missed entirely.

I waited to give her the opportunity to expound on her notion of who God is. When she said she couldn't think of anything else, I asked, "Do you see what is missing from your list? You didn't use any word that describes the mercy of God. You didn't call Him compassionate, loving, or faithful. You didn't identify Him as your heavenly Father. Frankly, your God is a God who demands performance from you. His standard is perfection, and you're depressed because deep down you know you can never measure up."

To help her embrace the understanding that God is also a loving father, I asked her to picture herself playing little league baseball with

God as her father sitting in the bleachers. I said, "Imagine you just hit a grounder to the shortstop, and it's bobbled. You run to first base as the shortstop's throw sails over the first baseman's head. You dash for second base and then head to third as the right fielder picks up the ball and throws it into the infield. You round third and zoom for home, sliding in safely as the second baseman's relay throw goes wildly over the catcher's head. You and I know that you didn't hit a home run. You should have been out several times! But this is little league—any parent in the stands is going to be screaming, 'Atta girl, you hit a home run!'"

Here's the analogy to Vanessa's struggle in her faith.

Her Bible study and prayer time may not be major league stuff right now. She may, in fact, be in little league. Her best efforts at praying and studying the Bible may be nothing more than grounders to the shortstop, but God knows her heart—just as He knows your heart. If an earthly parent would proudly cheer his little leaguer's efforts from the stands, how much more would your Father in heaven love and cheer you on, too?

What's this got to do with your marriage makeover?

Plenty.

Like Vanessa, you're probably wrestling with the feeling that God wants to zap you because your marriage is in trouble. You may feel that He's like an angry, impatient judge peering over the top edge of His glasses with contempt because your faith is weak right now. You think the verdict is in and you don't measure up. Let me assure you that nothing could be further from the truth. The truest thing about God is His love and compassion for you—just as you are.

The second inadequate view of God that limits us is a wrong view of His love. Much like a broken record, I've heard this rationalization about God countless times: "Since God is a loving God, I can't believe He wants me to be unhappy. I'm miserable in my marriage and can't take the pain anymore. I refuse to believe that God wants me to continue living with this heartache, and I'm sure He wants me to get divorced."

The limitation of this theology is that those who use it invariably don't see God as an awesome God with endless riches, power, and might at His disposal. This apparently was the problem of the Christian believers in the town of Ephesus. They felt the pain. They knew the hurt, but they didn't seem to know about the resources of God. Paul writes, "I pray also that the eyes of your heart may be enlightened in order that you may know the hope to which he has called you, the riches of his glorious inheritance in the saints, and his incomparably great power for us who believe" (Ephesians 1:18–19).

Do you see what the Lord offers?

Hope, riches, power!

In practical terms, God has provided these resources to you and to all who believe in Jesus. There is an alternative to divorce. God freely and generously provides hope, riches, and power for a couple who is willing to seek His face for their marriage. Talk about wonderful news! The question remains, how do we grasp hold of these good gifts? Read on.

TAPPING INTO HOPE, RICHES, AND POWER

When I first saw Steve and Roxanne, they were embroiled in a seriously hopeless marriage. I asked, "What is the most obvious problem in your marriage?"

With an angry jab of his finger, Steve pointed in the direction of his wife and said, "Roxanne is a liar!"

31

I said, "Really? What makes you think that Roxanne is a liar?"

"Before I married her," Steve said, "some of my friends urged me to ask Roxanne about her background. When I asked Roxanne, she told me, 'Babe, there's nothing about my past that would interest you. Don't worry about what your friends are saying to you.' I accepted her word and we got married. After we were married, however, I learned that Roxanne had been a prostitute."

I could feel his anger rising as Steve continued. "Roxanne knew exactly why my friends asked me to check into her background, but she didn't think it was a good idea to tell me what my friends already knew. George, how would you feel if you learned after your wedding that your wife had been a prostitute and some of your friends had had sex with her? I went nuts. I was determined to hurt her like she hurt me, so I told her that I had had an affair after we were married. I didn't really have an affair. I just wanted to pay her back for what she did to me."

At this point Roxanne interrupted Steve, asking, "George, how am I supposed to know which lie is true? Is he lying about having an affair or is he lying about not having an affair?"

How much hope would you have for Steve and Roxanne's marriage? Could your marriage survive betrayal, deception, and prolonged verbal attacks? I used all the best stuff I had learned from my PhD work; I called upon all that I had received in my seminary training, but the truth of the matter was that I knew I was in way over my head. If there was any hope for Steve and Roxanne, it was well beyond what I could give.

They needed hope and riches and power that I could not provide. But I knew where to find what they needed. Over several months I worked with them to apply the hope, riches, and power that are found only in the Bible. Guess what? Fifteen years later, Steve and Roxanne are deeply in love with each other. What happened?

While the counseling techniques probably helped some, this couple prayed and took hold of the riches and power of God. Along the way, Steve had come to see that God had already humbled Roxanne. Her sin drove her to have a relationship with Jesus. Steve may have viewed her as a liar and a prostitute, but God saw her as a precious daughter who loved Him.

Today, Steve insists he was the one who was totally wrong. He acted like a spoiled brat. His arrogant behavior toward his wife was a far cry from how Jesus would have handled the matter. He marvels at the great patience and forgiveness God has for his misbehavior. Steve now thanks the Lord every day for a wonderful wife who loves him and, more importantly, who taught him the meaning of the word *forgiveness*.

By contrast to the filth and venom he spewed in our first session, Steve speaks of Roxanne in only the sweetest of terms. What's more, this couple whose marriage was once in serious jeopardy now helps other couples in troubled marriages find happiness. You might be thinking, "Yeah, but HOW did they tap into God's offer of hope, riches, and strength?"

I'm glad you asked.

The answer is found in Ephesians 3:16–21 where Paul provides a three-step prayer to model:

1. PRAY FOR STRENGTH.
2. PRAY FOR LOVE.
3. PRAY FOR FULLNESS.

We need divine strength to sustain us in the midst of the crisis, we need to know the vastness of the love of God, and then we can be full of God's presence. Let's take those one at a time.

PRAY FOR STRENGTH

The benefits of praying for strength should be obvious to anyone in a hurting marriage. Every day, every ounce of energy is required to cope with the raw emotion and constant pain. What ultimately kills a bad marriage is the pain, which drains every last ounce of life from a couple. I've found that Christians in particular put up with a lot from their spouse for a long time before seeking help. But after they've been miserable over an extended period of time, eventually they come to the point where they say, "I don't think I can take this pain anymore. I am tired of hurting."

If the pain is especially acute, you are likely to think, *I can't believe a loving God would want me to be miserable the rest of my life. I have got to get out of this marriage.* Perhaps you know what it's like to wake up every morning with an ache in your gut. You get dressed knowing full well that there is nothing but misery and heartache awaiting you throughout the day.

When your pain is at its unbearable worst, invariably some well-meaning Christian will discover that you're contemplating getting a divorce and will say, "You can't do that. God hates divorce." Initially, you heed the reminder, but it only makes you feel worse because it doesn't make the pain go away. You do your duty some more. You try to behave . . . but you're dying on the inside.

In institutional religion, there is an assumption that if you want to belong to God or to the religious order, you need to behave, then believe, and then you get to belong. However, if we understand the essence of what Jesus taught, that message is exactly backwards. The right order is this: If we belong to Jesus—in other words, if we've invited Him into our hearts—we will believe; and if we believe, we will behave.

If we try to behave before we belong, it leads to legalism and burnout. We will become like my accountability partner, Mike, who was tired of always doing the right thing. Can Christians emphasize behavior over a right relationship with Jesus? Of course we can. That's why Paul says we need to pray for inner strength.

In fact, Paul addresses Christians in the city of Ephesus when he says, "I pray . . . that Christ may dwell in your hearts through faith" (Ephesians 3:16–17). That line begs a question: Doesn't Christ already dwell in the hearts of Christians? Is Paul assuming that the Ephesians are not believers? No, Paul calls them "the saints in Ephesus, the faithful in Christ Jesus" (Ephesians 1:1). He knows that they are believers.

So, what is Paul praying?

The Greek word *katoikeo* (most of the New Testament portion of the Bible was originally written in Greek) that is translated as *dwell* means to take up permanent residence. The idea here is that there is a difference between having Jesus in our lives and allowing Jesus to control our lives. Paul explains this another way in 1 Corinthians, chapter 3, where he acknowledges that Christians can be carnal—in other words, they believe in Jesus but allow all of the "stuff" of life to dominate their lives. Paul insists that when we are feeling weak and hopeless, we need to pray for inner strength, which comes from the indwelling presence of Jesus.

PRAY FOR LOVE

I came to a rude awakening a number of years ago. I was planning to preach on love, and as I prepared my message, I got the clever idea to interview my nine-year-old son. I planned to tape my son answering several questions on love and then play his responses on Sunday morning.

With my tape recorder in hand, I asked my first question, "Son, how do you know that I love you?"

Even as I asked the question, the thought crossed my mind, *Oh, this is going to be so good!* I was shocked when without the slightest hesitation my son said, "Dad, I don't know that you do love me!" I was stunned. I was numb with disbelief. How could my son, whom I loved so much, say he didn't even know that I loved him? Forget about the tape, I had some soul searching to do. That afternoon it occurred to me that if I say I love my son, but he doesn't feel it, what good is my love? That led me to wonder whether or not my wife and daughters knew that I loved them.

Fast forward to Valentine's Day. I decided to ask my family to write on my card how I could love them the next year in a way that would feel like love to them. My wife wrote, "I will know you love me if this next year you tell me more often, 'I love you.'" I thought, *How hard would that be? I can do that.* And I gladly committed myself to the task. On regular occasions I told her, "I love you."

As the next Valentine's Day drew near, I was looking forward to hearing her say, "Atta boy!" Instead, she wrote on her card "This next year I will know you love me if you say the words 'I love you' more."

I was devastated.

I thought, *I can't win. What do I have to do to please my wife? Enough is never enough.* I was sure tempted to prove that I say the words *I love you* far more than most men say that to their wives. But a new thought hit me: Don't make the same mistake you made with your son. Again, it didn't matter if I thought I loved my wife. What mattered was if my wife knew I loved her. I dedicated my efforts to learn how to love my wife in ways that were not natural for me. I had to love her beyond my comfort zone.

Today, after thirty years of marriage counseling, I have discovered that I am not unique. Every troubled marriage follows the same pattern: One partner may feel that the other is not meeting his or her needs, or may think, *I don't believe my spouse loves me.* That realization causes pain. It hurts to know that we are not loved. When the pain continues, we protect ourselves the only way we know how. We build a wall and insulate ourselves from our spouse to avoid the verbal or emotional barbs that rip away at the fiber of our marriage.

When the wall is thick and high enough, we conclude that we don't love our spouse anymore. We announce that the feelings are gone, and we may even say we doubt that we ever loved him or her. If we are believers, that leads to an overwhelming sense of hopelessness and despair. Unless something changes, we're well on our way to the divorce court.

That leads me to ask this question. Do you really know what "feels like love" to your spouse? Even if you think you do, have you ever asked? If not, I've found that the following steps are helpful in making sure we are getting this right.

- ASK YOUR SPOUSE, "HOW DID YOU FEEL MY LOVE FOR YOU THIS PAST WEEK?"
- ASK, "HOW CAN I PRAY FOR YOU TO GROW CLOSER TO GOD THIS NEXT WEEK?"
- PRAY, THANKING GOD FOR THE WAYS THAT YOU HAVE BEEN ABLE TO SHOW LOVE FOR EACH OTHER.
- PRAY FOR YOUR FAMILY, ASKING GOD TO HELP YOU GROW NEARER TO HIM IN THE SPECIFIC AREAS THAT YOU EACH IDENTIFIED.

PRAY FOR FULLNESS

After praying for His strength while the Lord is divinely at work in your relationship, and after praying for new insight into loving your spouse in a language that is clearly understood, the third prayer focus is to be filled with God's Spirit. You might be thinking, *Wait a minute. How can Christians drift from being close to God?* By our attitude and our actions.

Paul warns that it's possible to grieve the Spirit of God (Ephesians 4:30) through our "bitterness, rage and anger, brawling and slander, along with every form of malice" (v. 31). Likewise, he encourages us: "Be joyful always; pray continually; give thanks in all circumstances, for this is God's will for you in Christ Jesus. *Do not put out the Spirit's fire"* (1 Thessalonians 5:16–19, emphasis added).

What happens when we are upset with our spouse? We become angry. That anger can lead to bitterness. Unwittingly, we start telling our friends and family how poorly our spouse has treated us. That judgment leads to more bitterness as our friends and family conclude with us what a jerk he or she is. That in turn leads to more hopelessness and despair.

But what about Paul's charge to "be joyful always; pray continually; give thanks in all circumstances"? How do you do that when you are miserable? If left up to you alone, you probably can't manufacture those attitudes. You need inner strength. You need to know and grasp how wide and long and high and deep the love of Christ for you is. You need the Spirit of God to supernaturally change the attitude of your heart!

That was my advice to Mack and Hanna. In our first meeting, Mack confessed that he didn't love his wife anymore. He was pretty sure he was in love with a woman at work who knew how to love him in a way that felt like love to him. Hanna spoke only in whispers as she struggled to get any words out. She was obviously devastated to discover that her worst fears about his affair had been confirmed.

I shared some of the powerful stories with them about what I had seen God do in marriages that faced challenges as difficult as theirs. Then I said, "I want you to pray with me that God will touch you individually and touch your marriage. I don't know when that will happen, but when it does, you will have inner strength that gives you hope to go on." We set up our next appointment and then concluded in prayer.

As they arrived for the next session, they were a different couple. They were exuding hope. Joy had replaced despair. My curiosity soared. I said, "What happened to you?"

In concert they said, "God touched us."

Mack said, "God showed me the error of my thinking and gave me the inner strength to commit to my wife."

If I didn't say it, I sure thought, *This is too easy! I haven't given you my best counseling tools yet.* But there was no mistake. In one short week, God had so filled that couple that they were well on their way to recovery. I have often thought since then how nice it would be if all Christians could experience such a radical change so quickly.

Going back to my opening story of Mike, my accountability partner, who had announced that he didn't love Jan anymore: Remember how I told him that he needed the power of God? I know I prayed and I trust that he prayed, too. But for months nothing happened. He and his wife even separated for awhile. But we kept praying. In his case, healing took longer. Eventually, however, Mike was able to say to me, "Jan is my best friend. We still have some things to work out but we are going to make it!"

Not surprisingly the healing of Mike's marriage coincided with his renewed commitment to follow Christ. He had come to the point where he wasn't reading the Bible as he had in the past. He felt like a hypocrite when he prayed, so he prayed very little. He went to church but found little joy in worship. He needed the hope, riches, and power available from God through a closer walk with Him.

Looking back, I wish I could have done something to help Mike receive these gifts sooner. But only he could work out his personal relationship with Christ.

Do you desire to experience a real marriage makeover? Stop waiting for your spouse to shape up, and instead, start with yourself. Why not draw an imaginary circle on the floor? Pray that God begins a revival in that circle and then step inside and watch what happens.

THE ONE THING

Read this adaptation of the marvelous benediction Paul provides in Ephesians 3:20–21. Reread it daily this week:

> Now to him who is able
> Now to him who is able to do immeasurably
> Now to him who is able to do immeasurably more
> Now to him who is able to do immeasurably more than all we ask
> Now to him who is able to do immeasurably more than all we ask or imagine,
> Now to him who is able to do immeasurably more than all we ask or imagine, according to his power that is at work within us,
> To him be glory . . . Amen.

CHAPTER 3

ATTITUDE IS EVERYTHING

A fundamental assumption in America today toward a bad marriage is that the best way to stop the pain and experience peace is through divorce or separation. Oftentimes there is a euphoric peace that a partner enjoys when leaving the marriage. Why? Peace and a sense of well-being is a result of ending the conflict by avoidance. Coming home and not facing the one responsible for your pain anymore is, in fact, peaceful.

But will it last? Is it God's peace?

Many have told me that they think that it is.

Years ago, a young couple came into my office. Both husband and wife had attended the church where I had been the pastor for some time. When asked why they came to see me, Sarah said, "I don't love Bruce anymore." As I pressed her to elaborate on her feelings, Sarah confessed, "I've found someone else. Actually, I'm in love with Bruce's uncle. He's so caring and genuine. I feel good when I am with him and he knows how to meet my needs."

Both Sarah and Bruce were Christians, so I asked Sarah a direct question, "What do you think Jesus thinks about what you're doing?"

She said, "I know that what I'm doing with Bruce's uncle is wrong, but I just can't imagine staying married to Bruce. We fight all the time. Neither of us is ever happy. There is no peace in our home and I just can't take the yelling anymore."

I countered, "If you think that what you're doing with his uncle is wrong, how can you continue to do it?"

She said, "I believe God is a loving, merciful God. I can't believe He wants me to be as miserable as I am in my marriage. Besides, He's a forgiving God. I believe even if what I do is wrong, He'll forgive me!"

What is Sarah's main desire? She wants peace. She wants happiness. And she can't imagine experiencing them with her spouse. Look, I don't blame someone for wanting peace and happiness in marriage, especially if the marriage is one where conflict or verbal abuse is as predictable as the rising sun. But avoidance solves nothing. Perhaps the hardest thing I face in counseling is getting a couple to hang on and wait for God to give them the peace that they never imagined was humanly possible.

Sadly, far too many are impatient; they want peace at any price— and they want it *right now*. After all, they are a part of the "Microwave Generation." They are accustomed to the speed of text messaging and overnight mail. They are used to getting what they want, when they want it. And when the world around them is telling them that their best avenue to happiness is either a separation or a divorce, they long for peace so badly that they take the "instant" route to finding tranquility. What they experience may, in fact, feel peaceful. But is it God's peace?

No. But thankfully the apostle Paul, who had his share of unrest and persecution, tells us how we can have the peace of God even in the midst of conflict (Philippians 4:4–9). God's peace does not come from avoidance or from running. It's a peace that springs from a right attitude toward the Lord first, then toward people, and finally toward our circumstances.

Now, I realize what you're about to read may seem counterintuitive. You might think Paul's advice is ridiculous. Trust me. Because I've worked with hundreds of couples, I can attest to the fact that the peace Paul promises (whenever we trust God with our pain) runs deeper than any quick fix that might come from avoidance.

Paul writes that you and I should, "Rejoice in the Lord always." He adds, "Let your gentleness be evident to all. . . . Do not be anxious about anything" (Philippians 4:4–6). The extent to which Paul expects us to go is rather striking. He says to rejoice *always* . . . do not be anxious about *anything*. His charge is all-inclusive! There are no exceptions, even for a bad marriage.

Watch what happens when we follow this approach. Paul says if you do all of these things, the result will be that "the peace of God . . . will guard your hearts and your minds in Christ Jesus" (v. 7). Let me walk with you through this process.

THE FIRST STEP TO PEACE: REJOICE ALWAYS

In Philippians 4:4, Paul urges us to "Rejoice in the Lord always. I will say it again: Rejoice!" Rejoice always. That seems a bit unrealistic, doesn't it? How can we rejoice always, or even be joyful for a few minutes, when it seems that nearly every time we turn around our marriage partner disappoints or hurts us or betrays our trust? Our immediate response is to think, *Certainly Paul meant to say, "Rejoice* most *of the time."* After all, who can rejoice when your spouse rejects the gift of love that you offer so willingly and freely?

How could Paul tell us to rejoice always?

Paul was no dummy. He knew that the Christians living in the city of Philippi were struggling to maintain a constant level of joy and peace in their lives. Paul demonstrates that many in this church experienced seasons of joylessness because they tended to have a selfish, critical spirit (Philippians 2:3–4). Paul also knew that in the church, at home, or at work, we naturally have the desire to see things go our way. However, practically speaking, if our sense of inner peace depends on a need for everything to go our own way, we will never be able to "rejoice always."

Consider Kevin. Kevin was a lay caregiver in our church. In fact, he was the chairman of a ministry to help those in need within our church. He was at my side when we challenged his brother not to give up on God or his marriage. It didn't help. His brother got a divorce anyway. A few years later, I sat in the same room as Kevin told me that he, too, did not love his wife anymore and wanted out. When I urged him to seek help, he said, "I have chaired our caring program. There is nothing anyone can tell me that I don't already know. The problem is that I don't love my wife anymore. I am not sure I ever really loved her. I just can't stand it anymore. I am tired of all the fighting and all the pain."

Kevin proceeded with a divorce and then married a woman who left her husband. While he might have experienced some measure of "peace" by leaving his wife, his actions created a nightmare for his two precious little ones, who now must grow up wondering why Daddy left Mommy for another woman. I'm confident that there will be days ahead in Kevin's life when the peace he achieved will leave him, especially as he reflects on and deals with the children he left behind.

Each of us faces times in our marriage when we don't feel "in love," when harsh words are spoken, or when we wonder what we ever found attractive in our spouse in the first place. What do you do with those feelings? How can you find peace and joy when you are miserable?

I find it interesting that Paul said to rejoice "in the Lord." Our constant joy is dependent on our relationship with Jesus, not how we are treated by those around us. Do you believe that? Do you see that if you lack joy and peace, it's not because of how your spouse behaves? If you lost your joy, the first place to look for it is in your attitude toward Jesus. More precisely, Paul says our attitude "should be the same as that of Christ Jesus" (Philippians 2:5).

So what was Jesus' attitude like?

He "made himself nothing, . . . he humbled himself, . . . and became obedient to death—even death on a cross" so that we could live (Philippians 2:7–8). According to Paul, if we have lost our joy, it is because we have not carefully considered what Jesus has already done for us. We make the mistake of allowing our circumstances, rather than our relationship with God, to define our attitude; and, in the process, we lose sight of peace. Paul's God-centered perspective reminds me of a few lines from this classic hymn by Helen H. Lemmel:

> Turn your eyes upon Jesus.
> Look full in His wonderful face.
> And the things of earth will grow strangely dim
> In the light of His glory and grace.[4]

Does this sound easier said than done?

Several years ago, an older couple attended a Bible conference in Colorado. Their children were grown, and they were facing the sunset years of their lives. Both were Christians, but neither had ever been outspoken about their spirituality. The conference's theme was "Looking unto Jesus." While coming to grips with the message of what it means to be sold out to God, they decided to give Him top priority in their lives. No matter what would happen in their lives, they'd follow the Lord fully, not halfheartedly. Before starting on their long drive back home, they prayed: Lord, we give you first place. We have lived too many years for ourselves. No longer! We have decided to spend the balance of our lives for You. No matter what happens, the rest of our days are in Your hands.

En route to their destination late that evening, a car swerved over onto their side of the highway, heading straight toward them. The husband jerked the steering wheel to the right, slammed on his brakes, and skidded down into a ditch. They finally came to a stop in the middle of a shallow ravine. As water began to pour into their car, they pulled themselves out of their windows and then stood on top of the car as the water passed by beneath them. Stunned, but so grateful to be alive, they embraced tightly and then began to spontaneously sing:

> Praise God from whom all blessings flow;
> Praise Him, all creatures here below;
> Praise Him above, ye heavenly host;
> Praise Father, Son, and Holy Ghost. Amen.[5]

As their voices trailed off, they looked up on the narrow bridge above them and saw a large number of people staring down in silent disbelief. Even one of the highway patrolmen had placed his hat over his heart as he listened to them sing. The onlookers remained speechless.

Suddenly the elderly husband was seized with the realization that even this could be used as a testimony to bring honor to God. With a twinkle in his eye, a smile on his face, and with a trembling voice he began, "You might have wondered why we called this meeting here today." And with that he proceeded to tell the onlookers about their decision to "look unto Jesus" no matter what.

Instead of complaining and succumbing to fear, and instead of allowing their frightful circumstances to dictate their attitude, this couple kept their focus on Christ. They, in turn, spoke openly for the first time of the Lord their God.

The first step to peace is maintaining the right attitude—and that is only possible when our attitude is rooted in the Lord. The second step is the need to be gentle to all, especially your spouse. Brace yourself. That biblical insight is precisely the opposite advice some Christian counselors are encouraging these days.

THE SECOND STEP TO PEACE: BE GENTLE

While living in Denver, I got to know Bart and Felicia. Bart was a leading salesman with the largest distributorship of his product in Colorado. Felicia was the daughter of a pastor and regularly participated in the church. She sang in our choir and led a number of women's Bible study groups. Unlike his wife, Bart didn't have a spiritual background; he didn't know the Bible the way that she did, and as a result, she put herself forward as the spiritually mature of the two.

As you might expect, the conflict caused a great rift in their marriage. They clearly needed help understanding their differences. Because our church had a connection to a seminary, Felicia decided to start counseling with a professor on campus. After a number of sessions, the professor recommended that she and Bart have some "hostility therapy"—that's when one spouse gets to vent on the other without interruption.

I was invited to attend the session to "hold Bart's hand." For the better part of an hour, Felicia told Bart what a big jerk he was. She fumed over every little offense he had committed in the marriage. She held nothing back, berating his manhood, his character, his faith in God. Keep in mind that neither he nor I was allowed to speak or defend him as she blasted away with both barrels.

I'm not making this up.

And to think that hostility therapy was supposed to help their marriage! If you rail on someone for an hour or more, and if you think about everything that's awful or wrong about them, I guarantee that you're not going to have peace. How could you? You've spent all of your energy zeroing in on your anger. Not to mention the great damage you would do to the relationship.

By contrast, if you follow the wisdom found in Philippians, namely, to focus on "whatever is true, whatever is noble, whatever is right, . . . whatever is lovely" (4:8), you can't help but experience peace and healing. That's a promise straight from the Bible. It says, "And the God of peace will be with you" (Philippians 4:9). Pause and imagine the implication of that reality for a moment. How could you and I not experience real peace with God at our side?

We have this crazy notion today that if you express the anger, dwell on the anger, think about the anger, that somehow it will help release the pain. It doesn't and it certainly didn't in this case. After this hostility therapy, Felicia continued her counseling relationship with this counselor who told her that she was a "deep-water fish" and that Bart was nothing more than a "shallow-water fish."

Furthermore, the counselor claimed this difference was the fundamental problem in their marriage. His solution? He advised Felicia that Bart would never be able to swim in the deep water where she was. She was totally incompatible with somebody that shallow . . .

and, oh, by the way, he (the counselor) happened to be a deep-water fish, too. Not long after giving her his counsel, she divorced Bart and married the counselor.

Gentleness, a Way of Life

Again the difficulty here is with the extent of Paul's instruction. All of us can be gentle to some or most people, but Paul reminds us to be gentle to all. If we need a lever to pry us into action, Paul says, "Let your gentleness be evident to all. The Lord is near" (Philippians 4:5). Left alone we might want to mumble and grumble. Left alone we are often powerless and hopeless, but if Jesus is near, all of that changes.

Paul knows, however, that what he's exhorting us to do is difficult. In chapter 4, he urges two ladies who were active in the church to get along with each other. When I read verse 2, I was struck by the fact that the only reason we know about Euodia and Syntyche is because they were at odds with each other.

Showing a little kindness from person to person is more impressive than claiming vast love for all mankind. Most of us would say that we love people in general. It's the Euodias and Syntyches that bother us—that one person at work or in our family that rubs us the wrong way.

When some Euodia has upset us, we rationalize that we are justifiably disturbed because we were unfairly treated. We dwell on how disappointed we are until we get to the point where that one person dominates our thoughts. Each time we think of him or her, we become a little more bitter about how we have been wronged.

Josh was an elder in my first church. He loved Jesus and he especially loved the Bible. He just did not particularly like me. One day with his wife by his side, Josh confronted me: "Pastor, I can tell by the way you preach that you do not love God or the people of this church—or even yourself! I will not actively seek to oust you as our pastor, but I will support any movement to have you removed."

Naturally, I was startled by his hostility. Who wouldn't be? As he continued airing his grievance, I learned he was upset over the fact that a man named Bill had left our church earlier that week; he was sure I was the reason why. What Josh and his wife didn't know was that Bill had been giving drugs to a deacon's son. That deacon had privately challenged Bill to stay away from his son. Bill, who was disappointed with himself, attempted suicide. Contrary to what Josh thought, I had been with Bill several days that week. In fact, one evening I was up all night with him.

Bill had not stopped coming to our church because of me. I knew that for a fact. However, in order to protect Bill, I couldn't say anything to Josh. Boy, did I want to tell Josh how wrong he was. Instead, I listened without comment to his complaint. After that, every time I saw him and his wife at church, I walked down the other aisle. I honestly had no desire to shake their hands or have anything to do with them.

Philippians is my favorite book of the Bible. As much as I desired to avoid Josh and Sue, I couldn't get away from the command to be gentle to all. That obviously included this couple! As I was complaining to the Lord about how I could not possibly do what this text says, I discovered that the Lord was, in fact, near. He led me to a poem titled "Outwitted" by Edwin Markham that changed my attitude.

> He drew a circle that shut me out,
> [Rascal, scoundrel,] a thing to flout.
> But love and I had the wit to win;
> We drew a circle that took him in.

It was too obvious. I needed to love Josh and his wife. You say "Hi" to people you love. You go across the room and hug people you love. You invite people you love over to dinner and out to play racquetball. You speak well of people you love. There was a part of me that resisted, but I knew what I had to do. I invited Josh out to lunch and to play racquetball. I asked about his work and family regularly. We never became best friends, but we did spend time with each other. As I remember, I was always the one who initiated the contacts, but I persisted.

After serving that church for seven years, the Lord moved us to Colorado. Josh came to my farewell and waited in line to greet me. When it was his turn to say good-bye, he said, "George, you know I have not always appreciated your style of ministry, but I do want you to know that I have come to appreciate you as a friend."

I was tempted to blame Josh for my pain.

I was ready to focus on how he had become my enemy.

I now know that would have been a path to disaster.

It's all too easy to blame another person for our misery. We start by complaining: I am not happy in this relationship. The more we whine, the more miserable we become. We can even delude ourselves into thinking someone has stolen our happiness. Let's admit it—only when we stop blaming will we start enjoying health and happiness again. If we can own the mess we're in and trust the whole matter to God while we work with Him on our attitude and responses, there is hope. As long as we blame others, we remain a victim.

THE THIRD STEP TO PEACE: DON'T BE ANXIOUS

Let me guess what went through your mind when you read that heading: *Right, George. My world is upside down, I'm about to lose everything, I'm hurting, alone, afraid . . . and you're telling me, "Don't be anxious?" As if that's humanly possible!* The truth is, those are not my words. Those are the very words of God as recorded by the apostle Paul.

Before you get impatient with the discussion, stay with me on this. Paul's ultimate desire is for you and me to enjoy God's peace. Real, thirst-quenching peace. That's why he writes, "Do not be anxious about anything, but in everything, by prayer and petition, with thanksgiving, present your requests to God" (Philippians 4:6). Notice what happens if we do: "And the peace of God, which transcends all understanding, will guard your hearts and your minds in Christ Jesus" (v. 7).

Is this wishful thinking? Has Paul lost all sense of reality? Would Paul's instruction be different if he were in your shoes? What would Paul say if he had a long list of reasons to be discouraged—such as sickness, bills, a spouse who doesn't love him, the feeling that he's just no good, the misconception that God doesn't care about him, or even the thought that maybe his family would be better off if he were dead?

The truth is that Paul did have a serious list of reasons to be discouraged. He had been stoned by an angry mob. He had been shipwrecked three times. And, as he writes this letter, Paul isn't sipping iced tea in a hammock. He's in a Roman prison awaiting what he knew could be a death sentence. His friends at Philippi had just informed him that there were men preaching out of envy and deceit, hoping to stir up more trouble for Paul. Paul is about to die, so-called Christians are lying about him, and he still says, "Do not be anxious."

How do you find peace in a prison cell?

How do you find peace in a bad marriage?

Paul says, "I know what it is to be in need, and I know what it is to have plenty. I have learned the secret of being content in any and every situation, whether well fed or hungry, whether living in plenty or in want. I can do everything through him who gives me strength" (Philippians 4:12–13).

What is the secret of contentment?

How can I have peace no matter what I'm experiencing?

By turning to the One who is able to give us strength. That's number one. Second, we should guard our minds—in other words, while it is very difficult to control what we feel, we can control what we think. If we feel sad, we can't command ourselves to be happy and expect joy to immediately flood our being. However, if we do what Paul has been encouraging us to do, namely, to focus on the things in life that are excellent and praiseworthy, we will eventually discover God's peace.

Christian counselor Norman Wright gave me a technique that wonderfully applies Paul's truth in this passage.[6] Norman recommends that whenever we are feeling blue, we should pull out a 3 "x 5 "card that has the words, "Stop. Think." on one side of the card and Philippians 4:4–7 on the other side. First read the words, "Stop. Think." Then turn the card over and read the Philippians text.

After reading these verses, give thanks for anything true, noble, right, and so on, that you can think of and then put the card away. If at a later time you're feeling bad, pull out the card and read, "Stop. Think." Turn it over again and read Philippians 4:4–7. Give thanks once again, but this time come up with a new list of items that are true, noble, right,

53

and praiseworthy.

You may not feel the peace of God immediately, but you will experience the promise of this verse in time. I should know. I have used this technique for about thirty years and have found that when I faithfully do what the Bible says, I find the peace I crave.

There are many reasons why we insist we can't be happy. We blame our spouse. We blame our family. We blame our job. We blame circumstances. Paul says if you are miserable, you don't have to be. The secret to a lasting peace rests in embracing the joy of Jesus. How?

> Rejoice in the Lord in all things;
> Act with a gentle spirit; and,
> Refuse to be anxious.

Perhaps one of the more difficult challenges to this advice surfaces when we talk with our partner. It's both tempting and easy to be mean-spirited in our conversations, which fuels our anxiety and makes rejoicing a distant prospect. How we apply these peacemaking principles to the way we communicate with our spouse is the next stop on our marriage makeover.

THE ONE THING

Take a few minutes to make your own "Stop. Think." card. Remember to place the words from Philippians 4:4–7 on one side and "Stop. Think." on the other. Use as often as needed this week.

CHAPTER 4

LOOK WHO'S TALKING

Leo Tolstoy is the author of two of the world's greatest novels, *War and Peace* and *Anna Karenina*. Tolstoy was, during the last twenty years of his life, "probably the most venerated man in the whole world."[7] During the twenty years before he died in 1910, an unending stream of admirers made pilgrimages to his home in order to catch a glimpse of his face, to hear the sound of his voice, or even to touch the hem of his garment. Every sentence Tolstoy uttered was taken down in a notebook, almost as divine revelation. Sadly, however, his wife and most of his children did not share the awe of these devotees.

Tolstoy and his wife started their marriage strong. Tolstoy married a girl he loved dearly. In fact, they were so happy together, they used to get on their knees and pray to God to let them continue their lives in such utter heavenly delight. Over time, Tolstoy didn't find continued happiness in his marriage and work. Convinced that there had to be a higher purpose, he sought a divine mandate for his life. Ultimately, he had a religious experience that led him to denounce his property and possessions.

One problem. His wife did not share his religious convictions or his newfound zeal. While he desired to spend more time with peasants, she did not wish to give up the good life with their rich friends. They grew apart as she became jealous of his time spent away from home. At one point in their relationship, she would dress up as a peasant and spy on his movements—even out in the woods.

As you might expect, this once intimate and loving couple started to have explosive arguments. She became so irrational and jealous, even of her own children, that she grabbed a gun and shot a hole in her daughter's photograph. She once rolled on the floor with an opium bottle held to her lips and threatened to commit suicide, while the children huddled in a corner of the room screaming in terror.

What did Tolstoy do?

For starters, he smashed their furniture. Worse, he kept a private diary in which he placed all the blame on his wife. He was determined that coming generations would exonerate him and put the blame on his wife for their failed marriage. Rather than seek forgiveness and healing, Tolstoy was obsessed with ensuring his legacy.

What did his wife do?

She tore the objectionable pages out of his diary and burned them. She, in turn, started a diary of her own in which she made him the villain. She even wrote a novel entitled *Whose Fault?* in which she depicted her husband as a fiend and herself as a martyr.

Why did these two people turn the only home they had into what Tolstoy himself called "a lunatic asylum"? Obviously, there were several reasons, including his failure to love her as Christ loved the church (remember, He loved the church so much He died for it on the cross) and her failure to submit to his leadership. Certainly, their meltdown didn't occur because they were unaware of the power of words. Few have ever been more gifted with words than Tolstoy. Nor was it their lack of culture or training. They had the best of both.

Rather, this man and woman who were once so in love forgot how to talk to each other; and when they did talk, they used their words as weapons instead of agents of healing. Their story reminds me that you and I can have excellent verbal skills and a wonderful education, but we may still lack the ability to talk lovingly to the people we say we care for the most.

Why is communication so difficult? Apparently, we don't know as much about talking and listening as we think we do. If you and your spouse are going to win in your marriage, learning when to speak and what to say are critical, not optional, skills. Let's start with the issue of learning when to speak. As you'll see, it's a two-part plan: Speak after you listen and after you think.

SPEAK *AFTER* YOU LISTEN

Learning to speak after you listen implies you were listening in the first place! You might want to read that again. Far too many of us view listening as the thing we do while we are waiting for our next opportunity to speak. And, as we listen in this halfhearted manner, we wrongly assume that we understand what we're hearing. However, as Norman Wright points out, most of us don't realize how difficult proper listening really is. Wright says:

> When you stop to think about all that's involved in getting your message across it's apparent why misunderstandings often

occur. Communication specialists point out that when you talk with another person there are actually six messages that can come through.

What you mean to say.

What you actually say.

What the other person hears.

What the other person thinks he hears.

What the other person says about what you said.

What you think the other person said about what you said.[8]

It is estimated that the average listener hears only about 20 percent of what is said—and retains even less! It is a bit disheartening to think that we can be so easily misunderstood. But it illustrates why communication is often hard work in marriage. We want our spouse to listen and to understand what we mean, and yet often we respond before we've listened.

Can you see how easily communication becomes filled with static? We're picking up a fraction of what our spouse is attempting to say while racing to respond, to defend ourselves, or to make a point of our own. In Proverbs 18:13 the author says, "He who answers before listening—that is his folly and his shame." Similarly, James, one of Jesus' close followers, writes, "Everyone should be quick to listen, slow to speak and slow to become angry" (James 1:19).

Allow me to describe a situation where I had to practice being quick to listen and slow to speak—not to mention suppressing the temptation to allow anger to get the better of me for being misjudged. When we lived in Colorado, I led a small group that met weekly in our home. At our first session I said, "As we close tonight, let's share some prayer requests." After several identified a number of concerns for prayer, I suggested, "Any of you who feel comfortable, please pray and then I will close in prayer."

Two weeks later, I noticed that a couple who had attended our first session hadn't returned. When I called to check up on them, here's how the exchange unfolded. I asked, "Are you guys okay? We missed you. I was wondering if we'll see you next week?"

Jacob, the husband, said, "No, we're not coming back."

"Why?" I asked.

"We can't come back because you think we are stupid."

"Excuse me? When did I say that you are stupid?"

"You must think we are stupid because you asked us to pray out loud," Jacob said. "We're not comfortable praying publicly, so how can we come back to the group? Soon enough everyone will realize that we can't pray and everyone will think that we are stupid."

At that point in the conversation, I had several choices to make. I could have argued with Jacob over what I had really said. I could have underlined the fact that I never said he and his wife were stupid, nor was that my style. Instead, realizing that I should only speak after I listened, I paused to weigh what Jacob was trying to communicate. Because I waited to speak, I was able to pinpoint the essence of his concern.

I answered, "Jacob, I'm sorry I gave you the impression that I think that you're stupid. I never intended to give you that message. Let me try again to say what I meant."

Do you see how such a response defuses the tension?

It didn't matter whether I had actually used the word stupid in the group setting with Jacob; that's how he felt. The best way to demonstrate my empathy with his fear of praying in public was to tell him about the first time I was asked to pray aloud in front of others. Here's the story I shared with Jacob.

When You Haven't Got a Prayer

At the age of seventeen, I had been invited to the Sadie Hawkins dance by a classmate I'll call Donna—she's the one who pinned me. As part of our date, she invited me over to her house for a spaghetti dinner, which she personally cooked. It was wonderful and I pigged out on the meal. As the dirty dishes were collected, her father slipped out of the room for a few seconds and returned lugging a four-inch-thick black Bible.

That sure got my attention.

A moment later Donna's dad made an announcement: "We're going to have devotions." He proceeded to read a lengthy passage and then made a number of comments—punctuated by frequent glances in my direction. With a thunk, he snapped the Bible shut. "Okay, now we're going to pray," he said. I felt a faint flutter in my heart as he added, "I'll start and then Mama, Jimmy, and Donna will pray. George, why don't you close us in prayer?"

Me? I'm thinking, *Close in prayer? You've got to be kidding me. What's that like?* Keep in mind that I came from a liturgical background, which is to say I only learned a few formulaic prayers. In fact, I knew exactly two prayers at that time, "Come Lord Jesus, be our Guest, let these gifts to us be blest," and The Lord's Prayer.

Evidently unaware of my discomfort—or, secretly savoring my apparent nervousness—Donna's father began to pray. He prayed for our president, our country, and about all of the problems of the world, the difficulties of life, and the challenges of this and that … he went on and on. I'm shifting in my seat while breaking into a full sweat. I'm thinking, *When is this guy going to get done and what in the world am I going to say when it's my turn?*

Next, Donna's mama prayed. This saint prayed for everyone under the sun: the cousins, the nephews, the kids, the aunts and uncles, the loved ones—*everybody*. A sweet prayer, really. I couldn't help but notice how the words just flowed off of her lips as she prayed. Naturally, I was worried that when it was my turn I wouldn't know what to say. For sure they'd discover I was an idiot.

Then it was Jimmy's turn. Jimmy, who I might add was about three years younger than I was, must have been some kind of a genius—his words were just so well chosen. He prayed for those less fortunate, for the missionaries in foreign lands—you name it and Jimmy covered it. Now my stomach got into the act by starting a rumble with my intestines. With the sweat literally dripping from my face, I was sure that even the angels in heaven were going to laugh when it was my turn to pray . . . especially after they heard what I had to say.

And, as my heart raced within my chest, Donna prayed. Her voice was tender, warm, and passionate; she was like an angel praying next to me. I marveled at how Donna was so comfortable in the presence of God. Clearly there was no intimidation whatsoever on her part. She talked with God as if she were talking with her best friend.

That put me over the edge.

With sweat cascading down my face, it was my turn to pray. My shirt was sopping wet with perspiration as if I had spent the night in a sauna. To this day I have no idea what came out of my mouth. I do know that my stomach was doing these little flip-flops as I eked out my words. Somehow, mercifully, I managed to get through my prayer.

I don't know how I ended it, but the people at the table must have known and, in turn, started to go about their business. Donna and her mom headed to the kitchen to clean dishes. Jimmy dashed outside leaving me alone with Donna's father. For my part, I kept my head bowed because I didn't want to look up and face anyone. Donna's dad said, "George, why not join me in the other room?"

With some effort, I rose from the table and wobbled into the living room. He directed me toward a sofa where I promptly sat down for what I thought was going to be the Grand Inquisition. I was there for about two minutes before I had to excuse myself; I darted out to the front lawn and promptly threw up!

As I shared this story with Jacob, I said, "Jacob, I know what it is like to feel as though you are the only one who is not comfortable praying out loud. I sure never meant to put you in that position. Besides, I'd just as soon you not throw up on my carpet! It's perfectly fine if you don't pray aloud. There are others in our group who feel the same way as you. Will you accept my apology and come back?"

Thankfully, Jacob and his wife did come back to my Bible study and were mainstays in our group from then on. You see, if Norman Wright is accurate, there are several implications about what we say:

- DON'T BE SURPRISED WHEN PEOPLE DO NOT UNDERSTAND WHAT YOU SAY.
- DON'T TRY TO DEFEND YOUR MENTAL AUDIOTAPE OF WHAT YOU "KNOW" YOU SAID.
- DON'T ACCUSE A LOVED ONE OF BEING A LIAR BECAUSE THEY DID NOT ACCURATELY REMEMBER WHAT YOU BELIEVE THEY SAID OR WHAT YOU THINK THAT YOU SAID.
- WHEN YOU ARE MISUNDERSTOOD, LOOK FOR THE OPPORTUNITY TO EXPLAIN AGAIN WHAT YOU REALLY MEANT TO SAY.

By way of summary, your goal is to speak after you have listened. Next, and equally important, is to speak after you think. As you'll see in a moment, I learned the importance of thinking before speaking the hard way.

SPEAK *AFTER* YOU THINK

Here's one for the books. Let me tell you about my first date with Joan, the woman who ultimately became my wife. This was back in the days when I desperately wanted to impress the girl who struck me as gorgeous, as intelligent, and as the kind of young lady I'd really like to develop a relationship with. Joan and I ventured out on a day trip to Caseville, Michigan. I had everything planned out. You see, we were going to spend a romantic afternoon on a beach by the lake. What could go wrong?

Plenty.

We got off to a rough start, thanks to my car.

Before we were even a mile from home, my trusty 1960 Chevy decided to drop the muffler. Without a muffler, the Chevy bellowed, belched, and blustered on par with a sonic boom. Not wanting to give up on the date, I pulled to the side of the road, kicked the muffler into the ditch, hopped back in the car, and started to improvise.

For the next hour or so, each time we approached one of the many little towns along the way, I had to accelerate before getting too close to town and then coast the main drag. That way I wouldn't have to rumble through. It was the Fourth of July, and I knew a lot of police were patrolling the streets. The last thing I wanted was a ticket for disturbing the peace.

Thankfully, we arrived at the beach without a police escort. We got our towels and chairs and found a spot to relax. The sun was piping hot; by all appearances we were in for a picture perfect day—that is, until it was time to leave. You see, I had been working in the construction trades and normally wore shorts and no shirt. As you might imagine, I had a pretty decent tan by July. To be roasting on the beach all day wasn't a problem for me, especially with a tan that would have made Coppertone proud.

For her part, Joan had worked at a soda fountain shop and was as white as vanilla ice cream. My date hadn't been exposed to the sun all summer and, with her fair complexion, quickly became beet red. In fact, Joan's sunburn was so serious, her body blistered up. She remained in pain from head to toe for a week.

With the sun starting to set, we packed our picnic and made the one-hour drive back to her home. Once there, I had to physically help her walk to the door—her legs were as straight and stiff as a starched shirt; her knees wouldn't bend. As we inched our way to the door, my mind raced. I thought, *Boy, I really like this girl. I really need to say something that demonstrates my compassion and tenderness regarding what she's feeling.*

So, as we were about to say our good-byes, I'm embarrassed to say that I blurted out a real doozy:

"Joan, do you feel as awful as you look?"

While that line seemed like the right thing for me to say off the top of my head, it didn't take long to figure out that I should have given a lot more thought to what I said before I had spoken. In hindsight, my comment was about as gentle as 60-grade sandpaper. As I learned the hard way, every time we utter a word without considering whether it will inflict pain or bring joy, we risk the very relationships we care about the most.

I'm confident that you can think of a number of times when your spouse wounded you with his or her words. But, can you think of something you have said that you regretted the moment the words left your lips? Can you pinpoint an insensitive comment you blurted out that might demonstrate a lack of forethought on your part? While all couples struggle in this area, I have discovered that those whose relationships have approached the near meltdown stage tend to speak more frequently without listening or thinking first.

In reality, great damage can be avoided if we just slow down long enough to consider and weigh our words before speaking them. Likewise, it is prudent to speak only after we think. Proverbs advises, "He who guards his lips guards his life, but he who speaks rashly will come to ruin" (13:3). Here's another good piece of advice from Proverbs: "He who guards his mouth and his tongue keeps himself from calamity" (21:23). On the surface, this guarding-of-the-mouth business seems easy enough. All we have to do is listen and think before we speak, right?

There's more.

Say What?

As I mentioned at the outset, communication is also difficult because often we don't know what to say. Again, in Proverbs we discover that there are three keys to successful communication:

speak helpfully—use words that edify
speak honestly—tell the truth in love
speak humbly—admit that the other person may be right

When we follow this godly advice, the words we speak will build up those who hear. And isn't that the goal? If you want to save your marriage, and if you desire to thrive in your relationship one day, it only makes sense to speak words that bring life. Proverbs 10:21 puts it this way: "The lips of the righteous nourish many, but fools die for lack of judgment." Similarly, Proverbs 15:2 states, "The tongue of the wise commends knowledge, but the mouth of the fool gushes folly." Verse 7 adds, "The lips of the wise spread knowledge; not so the hearts of fools."

It's hard to argue with this advice. There are times, admittedly, when it's difficult to find the right words or to say the right thing. This is especially true if others are agitating us or if extenuating circumstances catch us off guard. I should know. I've jumbled my words more than once. Case in point.

As a kid, I grew up in Flint, Michigan—which means I was raised in an automotive town and was naturally driven toward car collecting. For the longest time my eye was captivated by the Corvette convertible. Talk about a cool car! However, as I got older my affection shifted to the MGB Roadster convertible, a real beauty imported from Britain. Just my luck, my neighbor had two of them and was about to move out of state and needed to sell one.

I scraped together the cash and proudly purchased a candy-apple red, A-model 1974 MGB Roadster convertible. As I drove down the road, my life changed. People stared . . . some honked and whistled . . . kids gave me the thumbs-up . . . and, when stopping for a red light, strangers would frequently scratch out their name and phone number on a scrap of paper and throw it into my car. With a shout they'd say, "If you ever think of selling that, I'd really be interested in buying it." Here I was in my midlife crisis thinking I'm just the coolest thing in the world.

Naturally, I kept the car parked safely in my garage. Nobody drove it but me. One day my twenty-one-year-old daughter, Kathy, came home from college with Mark, the guy she was dating. I could tell that she wanted to impress her date, so she approached me with Mark at her side.

She put me on the spot when she asked, "Dad, can I drive the MGB?"

I swallowed hard. Nobody drives the MGB but me. She knows this. She's known it for years. But since I'm the pastor, I've got to be nice, right? What's more, Mark was standing there watching my every move like a video camera for the evening news. Had it been just my daughter, I would have put my foot down and said, "Come on, Kathy, you know

I can't let you do that." However, with Mark serving as an eyewitness, I felt there was no way I could embarrass my daughter.

After a long moment, I said, "Okay, Kathy, but I'm going to back the car out of the garage." I didn't want to take a chance of her doing any damage to my car. I backed my pride and joy out of the garage and got it pointed in the right direction on the street. Kathy got in the driver's side, and as she buckled up, I leaned over and said, "Now, honey, have a good time. I just want to remind you that this car is my baby, so please be careful."

She gave me one of those little smiles as if to say, "Dad, please . . . we're going to Blockbuster, which is, what, all of a mile and a half away? Chill out. We'll be fine."

As I learned later, Kathy eased into town and stopped for the red light at our one "major" intersection. The light turned green and she proceeded across the two-lane highway. She was almost through the intersection when an SUV on the cross street ran the red light. Kathy had no chance. He smashed right into the back of the MGB, spinning it around like a top. From the passenger-side door back, the whole thing was caved in.

Kathy called home crying. "Mom," she sobbed, "we've had an accident."

Joan asked, "Honey, are you okay?"

"Yeah, I'm okay. Mark's okay, too. But dad's car is pretty messed up," she said through her tears.

"Oh, he's not going to care about his car, as long as you're okay, that's all that matters."

After providing comfort and a listening ear, Joan came to tell me the news. She said, "Kathy's had an accident but she's okay."

Now, I did hear her say that Kathy and Mark were okay. But my first question was, "Well, how's the car?"

"Don't worry about the car, the important thing is that Mark and Kathy are okay."

I was immediately apprehensive because Joan didn't want to tell me about the car. Was it a scratch? Something that could be buffed out? Maybe a minor dent? Perhaps a busted headlight?

With these thoughts racing through my mind, I drove to the scene. Granted, somewhere in my brain I still had the message that Kathy and Mark were fine, but with one look at my car, I got sick to my stomach. I walked around that car like the children of Israel marching around the city of Jericho, kicking the dust. I didn't say a word. My jaw was too numb to speak. Meanwhile, Mark was embracing my daughter and she was weeping in his arms. For five minutes I didn't say a word to either of them. Then, with a grunt in their direction, I mumbled, "See you back at the house." With that, I turned and left.

Let's pause there for a moment.

While I didn't vocalize but one short sentence, my actions, my body language, and my facial expressions communicated volumes. I was visibly incensed. There was nothing helpful about my body language. No loving arm. No tender touch. No caring eye contact.

Nor did my actions communicate that I honestly still loved my daughter more than that heap of crunched metal. Worse, there was no way I was prepared to humble myself in front of my sobbing daughter and her boyfriend and admit I had the completely wrong attitude. In other words, contrary to the admonition of Proverbs to speak helpfully, honestly, and humbly—I blew it. Big time.

As I drove home, I had one of those "God moments" when I felt the scales fall from my eyes. The words of Proverbs echoed in my mind,

"Reckless words pierce like a sword, but the tongue of the wise brings healing" (12:18).

In the silence I thought, *I'm such a blockhead! There's your daughter, the fruit of your loins who has been devastated because of what happened to the car. You told her right before she left that the car was "your baby." You ridiculous fool. She's your baby—not some car.*

Upon further reflection, I had to wonder how I could have let this happen. Well, I allowed the MGB to become an idol in my life and to take the place of my family, to take the place of my God, to rule my emotions, and to rule me. By the time I got back to the house, I was heavily convicted. When Kathy and Mark came back, I apologized for ten minutes. By the way, while our insurance paid for the repairs, I was never able to drive the car again. I sold it because I had allowed something to take the place of God in my life.

Communication in marriage is often difficult because we tend to speak before we listen and before we think about the implications of our words. And communication can be difficult because we fail to speak helpfully, honestly, and humbly. How are you doing in this area? When you speak to your spouse, are you helpful or hurtful? Are you using words that edify or vilify? Do you speak the truth in love, or do you wield the truth like a weapon?

If, like me, you've blown it, the good news is that we can confess our failures with the realization that Jesus died for them. And because Jesus has forgiven all of our sins, we, in turn, should be gracious to others— especially our spouse. Yes, we need His strength to curb our tongues when we speak to one another. In fact, it is by His supernatural power that we can follow these commands in Proverbs. That said, in the next chapter I'll give you a number of tips and tools to have yourself a good, clean argument for those times when you really must hash things out.

THE ONE THING

Find Appendix A at the back of this book. This section contains what I call the communication date. You'll find a series of questions to help you reconnect conversationally with your spouse.

Why not meet for dinner or dessert this week for your first communication date. Don't forget to apply the tips and tools found in this chapter—namely, listen and think before you speak.

CHAPTER 5

HAVE YOURSELF A GOOD, CLEAN FIGHT

Gregg and Jill were experiencing a serious conflict in their marriage. He worked in the personal finance industry, and she was a stay-at-home mother of two children, ages five and six. In one of my early sessions with them, I asked, "Jill, from your perspective, what is the problem?"

"The problem is that Gregg doesn't love me," she said.

"What makes you think that he doesn't love you?"

"He just doesn't!"

"Jill, can you give me a specific example of a time when you felt that Gregg didn't love you?"

"Sure." Jill stole a glance at Gregg and then said, "Last week I had the day from hell with our children. They whined and complained all day long. They were loud. They were obnoxious. They were demanding.

After doing battle with them for the entire day, I was looking forward to taking a much-needed break when Gregg got home from work."

Even as Jill was retelling her story, I sensed her anxiety rising. It was as if she was reliving the stressful episode. Days like the one she was describing are extremely draining and a test of anybody's sanity.

Jill continued, "The second I heard Gregg's car pull up, our daughter spilled the glass of milk I had just poured for her. She started crying as she left me to clean up the mess. As I was mopping up the puddle on the floor, our son stood up on the kitchen table and grabbed the light fixture. When Gregg came in the door, our son was literally swinging back and forth from the light fixture like a monkey at a zoo."

I'm not making this up!

She said, "Gregg looked in our direction . . . milk dripping onto the floor and all. He had to see my haggard face. He couldn't miss his son acting like Tarzan. He certainly heard his daughter wailing. Instead of asking how we were—or offering to help—he grunted in our direction and walked right past us! He actually picked up the paper and went into the living room. He sat down to read as if there wasn't a disaster going on at all. How am I supposed to believe this man loves me when he could so totally ignore me . . . right when I desperately needed his help?"

I looked at Gregg and asked, "Do you love your wife?"

He answered firmly, "Yes, I do!"

"Do you remember the day that Jill just described?"

"I remember that day," Gregg said.

"Did you see your son hanging from the light fixture?"

"No, not really," Gregg said. "I took Jill's word for that detail, but honestly I'd had an extremely stressful day at work, too. I was fried. I fought with several clients. I argued with my staff. I had a mountain of work to do and didn't begin to get it all done. I couldn't wait to leave the office and come home where I could relax. I thought my home was a place of refuge. I guess when I came in, I just didn't notice Jill and the kids because I was too wrapped up in my own stress. I just needed some time to sit down with the paper and catch my breath before I could address another crisis."

Can you see the makings of their conflict?

Like many couples, Gregg and Jill are hardworking parents, each squeezed to the max. Both had legitimate needs and understandable expectations of their spouse. I don't blame Jill for thinking that Gregg didn't love her. He had been insensitive and acted in a way that made her feel unloved. Unfortunately, neither knew how to talk through conflict constructively, which is why they came to me.

In time, and with me serving as referee and coach, Gregg and Jill learned how to work through their conflicts rather than be crippled by them. You might be thinking, "Yeah, but George, we never fight in our home." That's possible. There are, after all, three types of people:

The "shouters"
The "pouters"
The "outers"

Briefly, the shouters have a one-size-fits-all approach to conflict: they shout. And, like a fistful of marbles hitting the floor, everyone scatters for cover once a shouter launches into a rant. As you can imagine, constructive, thoughtful dialogue isn't possible when people are yelling.

The pouters use the silent treatment when they are upset. Since they live in the delusion that they never fight or have any difficulties, they just keep their anger internalized. Instead of shouting, their displeasure or anger is expressed through the cold-shoulder treatment; the home may be less noisy, but their nonverbal actions can still wound. Like

Mount St. Helens, a day will come when the pressures, boiling under their placid façade, will build to the point of an eruption.

The outers, by contrast, have learned the secrets of a good, clean fight. They don't bottle up their feelings like the pouter, nor do they harangue each other with shrieks and shouts. Instead, they are committed to talking things out. They understand that conflict in marriage is inevitable; that the only place where we'll live without conflict is in heaven; and until then, they strive to resolve marital conflicts in a way that is consistent with the way Jesus said we should treat one another. How? There are, at least from my perspective, six rules for a good, clean fight. Let's look at them one at a time.

Rule #1: Remember, you are on the same team.

In Ephesians 4:25–32, Paul was writing to those who were bickering with one another in the church at Ephesus. Paul reminds them, "We are all members of one body" (v. 25). What does he mean by that? Christians are to be supportive and encouraging to one another with their choice of words. Paul goes a step further: "Do not let any unwholesome talk come out of your mouths, but only what is helpful for building others up according to their needs, that it may benefit those who listen" (v. 29).

Applying Paul's message to couples, the next time you face a conflict, stop and consider, *Is what I'm about to say going to build up my spouse . . . or tear down my spouse?* If for some reason your husband or wife has lost sight of Paul's advice and the conversation starts to get heated, why not gently remind, "Honey, we're on the same team—let's keep it that way."

Complicating our efforts to remain united is our assumption that we possess a computer hard drive in our heads. We make the mistake of thinking that our hard drive keeps a perfect record of everything that anyone has ever spoken. When the inevitable conflict arises, both husband and wife quickly review their memory files. Not surprisingly, two different versions of the past emerge. In turn, we get into an argument over what we both *think* was said, sometimes fighting over events that happened eons ago. Rather than trying to build each other up, the conflict shifts into a contest of wills: We want to win. We want to prove that "I'm right and you're wrong."

Talk about futile.

Couples waste a lot of time trying to prove whose version of previous events is the right one. The minute we say, "That's not what you said" or "That's not what happened," we invite a fight. Besides, who cares what is recorded on your hard drive? The more important point is that you are members of one another. To experience a fair fight, remember you're on the same team. Steer away from words, attitudes, and actions that intentionally divide your unity.

Rule #2: Check your weapons to make sure they are not deadly.

Years ago, Joan and I went on a family trip down to Muscatine, Iowa. I grew up in the state of Michigan, and until I moved to Iowa City, Iowa, I had never even seen the Mississippi River. Naturally, I had this fantasy of seeing Huck Finn floating down the river in Muscatine. At the least, I expected I was going to see a number of boats and a lot of exciting activity. After all, this was the Mississippi!

With the family in tow, we drove up and down the Mississippi near Muscatine for maybe ninety minutes and saw nothing remotely like the picture I had envisioned. Joan is a practical woman. She realized that driving alongside the Mississippi River for an hour and a half was not the most exciting way to spend a family day. Our children were preschoolers and needed to move. Joan consulted her map and then said, "There's a state park here called the Wildcat Den State Park. Why don't we go there?"

My body stiffened. Gripping the wheel a little tighter I said, "I'm sure we are going to see a boat if we just keep looking." I figured if we drove long enough we'd be sure to find something of interest—map or no map.

Several fruitless minutes passed when Joan rather gently and sweetly suggested, "You know, dear, we're real close to Wildcat Den State Park. It's just right over there, according to the map."

Finally, I relented. We drove into the Wildcat Den State Park parking lot and, at first glance, saw nothing. A bunch of trees beyond a deserted parking lot was about the extent of the excitement. As we got out of our Toyota, I was feeling disgusted with the events of the day. Of course, the kids did not care where we were. They just wanted to get out of the car. They were free.

However, I was thoroughly miffed. Why? My wife was the one who wanted to stop, and I wanted to keep up my search for Huck Finn. So, I was fuming and thinking, Wildcat Den—*right*. The only wild things here are the weeds pushing their way through the blacktop. In that moment of frustration and conflict, any number of hurtful things could have rolled off of my tongue. I could have unloaded on my wife with both barrels. I could have ripped into her with a few choice zingers.

Instead, I did the mature thing—I looked over at Joan and said, "We always do what you want to do!"

You'd think I would have known better. Almost as soon as the words came out of my mouth, I realized how utterly false and foolish they were. I couldn't believe that I said something so ridiculous after driving for an hour and a half while my family patiently endured my vain search for a boat on the Mississippi River.

I started laughing.

Joan started laughing, too.

After we talked through our feelings—mindful that we were still on the same team—we scouted around and discovered that Wildcat Den State Park is actually a beautiful place! Once we got on the trail, we encountered a deep ravine running though the middle of the park. Talk about absolutely breathtaking. For a moment I thought I had stepped into the Colorado Rockies.

And to think I got worked up trying to see a silly boat and had the nerve to say that Joan always had to have her way. You know, Paul says we need to speak the truth to one another, but we're also supposed to speak the truth "in love" (Ephesians 4:15). It is so easy for us to draw emotional judgments from feelings that we have and then say something that encourages a fight, which is why Paul writes, "Therefore each of you must put off falsehood and speak truthfully to his neighbor" (v. 25). Make that truthfully . . . and in love. In other words, when you encounter conflict in your marriage, check your weapons and make sure they're not deadly. Don't speak falsely, hurtfully, or out of spite. Rather, season the truth with love.

Rule #3: Agree together that the time is right.

I have talked to a number of couples who have faced the same dilemma that Joan and I have faced in our marriage. I love to talk and process things out loud. I am also a problem solver by temperament—an "expressive driver" according to the temperament tests. I like to fix things. As Joan could tell you, I've been working on fixing her for years. She doesn't need the help near as much as I do, but I try nonetheless.

Early on in our marriage when we were having any number of the arguments that young couples have, invariably I wanted to fix things right then. Joan was wise enough to recognize that you do not solve conflicts when you are emotional or angry. She would not talk or be drawn into a heated exchange. That used to drive me nuts. I could not handle it. There were times when I virtually bullied Joan into talking.

I actually came up with a buffet of wrong and hurtful accusations and judgments . . . I told her she was spiritually immature . . . that people of God worked out their problems, they didn't stick their head in the sand . . . if she loved Jesus, she would communicate because that's what believers do. I mean to tell you, I berated her with all of this nonsense trying to provoke her to talk when she wasn't ready.

You see, there's a right time and a wrong time to work through a conflict. The right time is after you've cooled down and are mindful of the fact that your spouse is not your enemy: he or she is on the same team. The right time is when you are able to be constructive with your comments, not destructive; when you've checked your words so that they don't wound.

The wrong time is when you're exhausted, angry, or haven't prayed for strength to be more selective with your word choice. It's the wrong time when you are feeling rushed, impatient, or if others are in the room, especially your children. And it's almost always the wrong time to hash things out in public.

There were occasions when all of my whining did get my wife to talk to me at what was the wrong time for her. Guess what? In badgering her, unwholesome words came out of her mouth. I didn't hear anything that uplifted my spirit or that made me closer to Jesus. In fact, I heard things that made me madder. Having done this enough times with Joan early in our marriage, I discovered how right Paul was in Ephesians 4:26, 27, and 29. He says that one way we give the devil an opportunity is when we allow putrid or rotten words to come out of our mouths. In those moments, we do not speak words that are good for edification, meet the need of the moment, or give grace to the hearer.

You can imagine what happens when we are angry. We say words that hurt and that we later regret. Keep in mind, Paul knows that we're human and humans become angry. Still, that's no excuse to fly off of the handle and bark a flurry of angry words at our spouse. Paul says, "'In your anger, do not sin': Do not let the sun go down while you are still angry, and do not give the devil a foothold" (Ephesians 4:26–27). By saying "in your anger," the clear implication is that God knows that He has made us as emotional beings. There are going to be times in our lives when we become angry.

In light of this reality, our goal is twofold.

First, we have to be able to say, "Time out; I can't talk about this right now." If you are like me, and you're the one who wants to talk about it, it's going to drive you nuts to establish that rule. But it helps prevent regrets, because otherwise unwholesome words will come out of somebody's mouth. Both husband and wife should have the ability to call a "time out." The reason for a time out is not to avoid the issue. It's to have some time to reflect on the real issue or issues.

It also provides space for us to get quiet before the Lord and get a handle on our emotions. We want to make sure we do not say something, ultimately, that we are going to regret. Joan and I have agreed to follow this guideline in our home now for about thirty years and have found that it doesn't take us long to calm down and be able to talk through our issues.

Second, while calling a time out is appropriate, so is calling a "time in." That's when, like two boxers in the ring, you agree to come together from your separate corners and roll up your sleeves for a good, clean fight. In the text it says, "Do not let the sun go down while you are still angry." Pastor Chuck Swindoll takes this verse literally and suggests that since most conflicts in the home happen after sundown, we can anticipate a shoot-out by the next sundown.[9] In other words, we have twenty-four hours to talk about whatever caused the conflict.

Rule #4: Remember that the aim of the fight should be edification.

Several years ago, Joan and I traveled to Indiana to bring our daughter, Michelle, home from college. Instead of taking something larger for the move, we drove Joan's Buick. It's funny how much stuff a college student can accumulate. By the time we loaded Michelle's belongings into our Buick and into her car, there was barely enough room in the vehicle for the driver. We had every nook and cranny jammed with stuff.

By the way, Michelle was driving a 1985 Chevy Cavalier. Honestly, it was the scourge of the church parking lot. This piece of junk had a dented back end. The struts in the front were completely shot, producing an interesting effect—the Cavalier would wave up and down at the oncoming traffic as she drove. Oh, and did I mention that the car's air conditioner didn't work?

That day was particularly warm, so I said to Joan and Michelle, "Why don't you two ride in the Buick together and I'll take the Cavalier." While they took turns driving the Buick, I was sandwiched into a steaming Cavalier for hundreds of miles. Yes, feel free to call me Mr. Wonderful. However, my act of self-sacrifice quickly disintegrated into a full-blown pity party. In fact, I didn't realize how much I was reminding both Joan and Michelle of my great sacrifice and how close I was to an argument until we got about halfway home.

With the temperatures rising and my countenance falling, Michelle finally spoke up. She said, "You know, Dad, in a psychology class I took at Taylor this year, we studied the principle of win-win."

"Oh, that's interesting," I said as I dabbed my forehead with the edge of my shirt.

"And Dad, one of the things we learned is that there are a number of people who sometimes develop a win-lose situation because they have a martyr complex. They offer to do something gracious and loving, but they never let you forget about it."

Do you see what Michelle did? Not only did she speak the truth in love, she made her comments in a way that edified me. Beyond that, she reminded me how much I needed to turn my predicament into a win-win situation by suggesting that I tune into a ball game.

She modeled something I've been preaching for years from Ephesians, namely, after you take a swing, offer a positive solution. Paul put it this way, "[Speak] only what is helpful for building others up according to their needs, that it may benefit those who listen" (Ephesians 4:29). In this case, Michelle's caring approach worked because she identified my need—to change from a win-lose to win-win attitude—and built me up with a positive solution—check out a ball game.

After feeling sorry for myself for the first four hundred miles in that wreck, she helped me see that I was free to listen to a ball game without interruption! As it turned out, my favorite team, the Detroit Tigers, was playing the Milwaukee Brewers. Since we were driving through Wisconsin the game aired on several stations. Now, I could be happy even in the heat—and Joan and Michelle could be happy in their air-conditioned comfort.

Rule #5: Work out your conflict with your spouse, not your friends.

When difficulties arise, one of the areas where couples make a giant mistake is in their conversations with other people. They talk about their conflicts, their arguments, or their issues in public. This is especially detrimental to the healing process when there's been an affair.

Let me speak specifically about that circumstance for a moment since it is such a typical scenario. Regardless of whether the husband or the wife had the affair, the one who is the "innocent party," in my opinion, can now cause great damage. How? By "confiding" in too many others while emotions and self-doubt are high. Such exchanges can quickly evolve into gossip.

I understand why they may want to talk with their friends. They've been devastated and devalued by virtue of the fact that their partner found a relationship outside of the marriage union. As such, their tendency is to discuss very private, personal details with their parents, their family, their spouse's brothers and sisters—you name it—and tell them what happened.

Conversely, for the "guilty party"—the person who had the affair—the last thing they want is for their spouse to go and tell their mom and dad or all of their friends what's going on between them. Naturally, that's terribly embarrassing for them, and it could discourage them from working on the marriage because their spouse is potentially belittling them in public.

Take, for example, Troy. He's had an affair, he's repented, but his wife, Lisa, has failed to guard her tongue. Troy is thinking, *I can't face Lisa's mom, our friends, or the people in our church again because she's told all of them about us. She's cut me off from everyone I care about.* This creates a greater sense of hopelessness for him because he feels that his failure has been exposed to the world.

Don't get me wrong. It's appropriate to have people pray for you. My advice is to ask God for wisdom and then carefully identify one, no more than two, confidants whom you can talk to and pray with. Fight the temptation to go to your husband's mom and dad and tell them everything that's wrong with him.

Remember, we're expecting God to heal this marriage. When He does, it's not to the advantage of these outsiders to know everything that happened between you two. Why not? While you have forgiven your spouse, your friends and family may have a more difficult time in making the forgiveness connection. In turn, your spouse may be blacklisted. Because your friends can't get over what he or she has done, they keep playing those old tapes over and over every time they see your mate. That's unfair. In the end, careless words can sow the seeds for future difficulty.

Whether the conflict or offense is as serious as an affair or something less dramatic—such as consistently running late to family functions, overspending, poor judgment, forgetfulness, or finance issues—work out your conflict with your spouse, not the neighborhood. That's the good advice found in Proverbs 11:13, "A gossip betrays a confidence, but a trustworthy man keeps a secret."

Rule #6: Heed the prompting of God when He nudges you to seek forgiveness and oneness.

Our goal is to have a good, clean fight and come out on the other side as closer friends, deeper lovers, and inseparable soul mates. But there will be times when you blow it. You'll lose your cool. You'll say words that sting or wound. You'll forget you're on the same team and, in turn, level hurtful charges against your spouse.

I know. I've done it far too often.

When we blow it, we can either play the blame game or we can seek forgiveness. Forgiveness leads to oneness and that (as discussed in a prior chapter) is the last thing the enemy of our souls wants us to experience. He's the author of confusion, brokenness, and strife. By contrast, God desires our marriages to thrive. He wants us to successfully navigate the misunderstandings that divide marriages and homes.

It takes courage to say, "Honey, I blew it. I'm sorry. Please forgive me." The problem is that most of us don't like to admit we've done anything wrong. When I am tempted to think that way, I am no different from the Americans polled by *People* magazine a number of years ago.[10] The editors asked, "How many sins a month do you think you commit?" Are you sitting down? The average American answered, "Four sins." That's not four sins a day, mind you—that's four sins a month!

Christians claimed they committed about seven sins a month. Seven sins a month? What's going on here? The problem is that practically no one thinks they're a sinner. Many think that we're all such good people, we can do no wrong. If we underestimate our capacity to be at fault or to sin against our spouse, we'll neglect our role in the pursuit of forgiveness. The end result will be continued conflicts rather than the restoration and joy we desire.

More importantly, when we fail to seek forgiveness, we actually "grieve the Holy Spirit of God" (Ephesians 4:30). Let me clarify what the Spirit of God means. Briefly, when the Bible speaks about God, you'll find references to God the Father, God the Son, and God the Spirit. That can be confusing since the Bible also says there's only one God. So what's going on?

I find it helpful to picture water as a metaphor for God. Water can be a liquid, a solid (like ice cubes), or a vapor (such as steam). Although different in their function, at the core all three are still water. That's an imperfect yet helpful way to see God, His Spirit, and Jesus His Son: different persons yet the same God.

That said, why is the Spirit grieved? Because we are literally ignoring the Spirit's power and the role of the Spirit to restore our marriages. By denying the Spirit, it's as if we're saying, "No thanks, God, we'll manage our conflicts on our own—thank you very much." Talk about ludicrous! No wonder the Spirit becomes grieved. In reality, I am convinced that a marriage makeover is impossible without the supernatural intervention of the Spirit.

That's why Paul urges us to "Be kind and compassionate to one another, *forgiving each other*, just as in Christ God forgave you" (Ephesians 4:32, emphasis added). Furthermore, because the Lord loves you and your marriage, I promise He will put His divine finger on those occasions where you need to own up to your mistakes and seek forgiveness. When He does, for the benefit of your marriage, your children, and your legacy, listen when His Spirit speaks to your heart.

As you're putting into practice some of the tools and tips for a good, clean fight, the next step is to study the blueprints for healing, which God graciously presents in the First Epistle of Peter. That's the subject of our conversation in the next chapter.

THE ONE THING

Copy these six rules—or rewrite them in your own words—onto a 4" x 6" card or sheet of paper. Tape them to the back of your bathroom medicine cabinet door. Every morning as you brush your teeth, these rules will remind you how to have a good, clean fight. If you'd like, use them as a "contract" with your spouse and sign it together. I am convinced that if there is a conflict in marriage that cannot be resolved, it is because we are breaking the rules.

Rule #1: I will remember that we are on the same team.

Rule #2: I will not use deadly weapons.

Rule #3: I will discuss disagreements when we both agree that the time is right.

Rule #4: I will remember that the aim of the fight is edification.

Rule #5: I will work out my conflict with you, not a group of friends.

Rule #6: I will heed the Spirit of God when He nudges me to seek forgiveness and oneness.

CHAPTER 6

BLUEPRINT FOR A MARRIAGE MAKEOVER

In American culture, many star-studded marriages end quickly. Actress Drew Barrymore and comic Tom Green split after five months, and singer Kid Rock and actress Pamela Anderson divorced after four months.[11]

No doubt: "Celebrity divorces are big business. . . . And they certainly are common. The year 2007 alone saw the breakups of Britney Spears and Kevin Federline, Paul McCartney and Heather Mills, and Reese Witherspoon and Ryan Phillippe."[12]

On the other hand, Forbes reports there are some one-time power couples who were married longer—on average for twelve-and-a-half years—"and the settlements reflect that. Case in point: Former television producer Marcia Murphey walked away with $150 million, or half her ex's fortune. . . . And the current divorce between basketball great Michael Jordan and his wife Juanita, married for nearly 18 years, could be the most expensive showbiz divorce ever."[13] Payout is expected to be more than $150 million.[14] These mega stars remind us that there is a cost when a marriage falls apart. Johnny Depp in an interview with *Movie Star Magazine* suggests that for him the cost was far more than economic. His parents divorced while he was a teenager. Depp attributes anger issues that he has had as an adult to the pain caused by the dissolution of his parents' marriage.[15]

Clearly, we desperately need a blueprint for marriage makeovers. I believe the apostle Peter, in 1 Peter 3:1–7, gives us a divinely inspired blueprint for your marriage makeover.

Here, Peter records six verses for the wife and one verse for the husband. *Wait a minute*, you may think. *Is Peter a male chauvinist picking on women?* Hardly. There has been much vain speculation about why there are six verses directed to the wives and just one verse for the husbands.

Briefly, some have quipped, "It's because women are six times harder to teach than men." Others have said, "No, it's because it is six times harder to live with men than with women." Actually, if there is a reason for the difference, in the Greco-Roman world of that day it was more difficult to live with men than with women because it was a male-dominated society. Wives didn't have as many options as their husbands would have had. In any case, thankfully God has not left us guessing about His grand design for marriage.

Here's another preliminary thought.

All of us face difficult circumstances and difficult individuals. So did Jesus. He, like us, suffered because of people and unjust situations. He was treated unfairly. He was falsely accused, slandered, and vilified. He demonstrated love and was met with hate. He even healed ten lepers and remained unthanked by nine of them. And to think I sometimes get miffed when my wife fails to say "thanks" when I take out the trash.

Listen. If Jesus experienced trials while on earth, why are we so surprised when we encounter rough sailing in our relationships? Disappointment and pain are part of the package in a fallen world. Jesus said, "In this world you will have trouble. But take heart! I have overcome the world" (John 16:33). Wow! No matter what your situation feels or looks like—hopeless, pointless, or beyond repair—Jesus has overcome the brokenness, hurt, and pain of this world and offers you His riches, strength, power, and might to overcome any obstacle or trial your marriage will face.

Talk about great news!

Contrary to the current cultural trend to cut your losses and run, the secret to lasting healing and joy is to follow His lead. After all, this carpenter Jesus was the Master Architect and Builder who framed the universe. As you review the blueprint for your marriage makeover, why not ask yourself: How would Jesus—not the critics— handle the hurt and disappointment that I face? What would He do to restore my marriage?

These thoughts form a backdrop for the suggestions that Peter makes. He begins by addressing the wives and then the husbands. We'll do the same.

BUILDING BLOCKS FOR WOMEN ONLY

Peter starts by addressing women whose marriages are not good ones. Specifically, these are marriages where the husbands are not passionate about Jesus. There may be two reasons for that lack of spiritual leadership on the part of the men. First, it's likely that these husbands are not believers at all. If so, he's speaking to women whose marriages are filled with tension, conflict, and even embarrassment.

Second, it's possible that these women are married to men who are supposed to be Christians, but they're not acting like it. The husbands are not doing what God would have them do. The wife, in turn, would love to change the behavior of her husband. However, considering the culture Peter is addressing, these wayward husbands would not be inclined to be obedient to a woman. So, she's stuck in a seemingly dead-end marriage.

If you were Peter, what would you say to a woman in that situation? Leave your spouse? Lecture him? Badger him? Here's Peter's advice:

> Wives, in the same way be submissive to your husbands so that,
> if any of them do not believe the word, they may be won over
> without words by the behavior of their wives . . .
>
> 1 PETER 3:1

What's this? Be submissive? How about a little lecturing once in a while? Nope. The wayward husband will not be won back through your words. Rather, your actions speak louder than words. Talk about radical advice. You see, the first of three building blocks for the wife is what I'm calling the "action block." In a moment you'll also build upon the "adornment block" and the "attitude block." Used together, these three building blocks will form a foundation for your marriage makeover.

1. The Block of Action

The first block—action—is illuminated by Peter when he says, "They may be won over without words by the behavior of their wives, when they see the purity and reverence of your lives" (1 Peter 3:1–2).

I find it interesting that the word translated as *see* is not the normal word for *see* as used by Peter in the original manuscript. This is a particular usage that describes fans watching an athletic event. Put another way, Peter is saying, "Don't kid yourselves, wives; your men are watching you. They're tuned into you with the same interest that they have when watching the Super Bowl. You may not think so, but they're really spectators who don't miss anything you do."

How is that a good thing? Because the fact that he's watching means you don't have to waste time on lectures, little comments, guilt trips, or other forms of verbal manipulation in hopes of getting him to change. If he will change, he'll change because your behavior and your actions are speaking louder than words.

So, how is this dynamic a building block?

You build on the action block when you are faithful to model right behavior and Christian living, when you remain plugged into your church and your women's Bible study group, and as you continue to read the Scriptures on your own and with your kids.

You see, every time you pray with your children at meals and at bedtime or engage in these other action-oriented behaviors, God's Spirit can convict your husband. Whether he is an unsaved man or a Christian who is not stepping up to his role as a spiritual leader, Peter tells us that it's your behavior—not your words—that God may use to draw your husband into a right relationship with Himself.

2. The Block of Adornment

The second building block is the adornment block. In 1 Peter 3:3, Peter writes, "Your beauty should not come from outward adornment, such as braided hair and the wearing of gold jewelry and fine clothes." What's wrong with fixing your hair? What is wrong with a little jewelry? Nothing. Do not misunderstand what Peter is saying. He is not saying there is anything wrong with physical beauty. Men are happy to have a beautiful wife. My wife was a beauty queen in Flushing, Michigan; she was on the homecoming court in high school. I am thankful for that. It's great to be married to someone who's beautiful.

But here Peter specifically advises a woman married to a husband who is disobedient to God. He knows her temptation to use her looks to woo her man. A woman in her situation might hope to control her husband, to get him to change, to get him to obey God, or perhaps even obey her with her beauty. Using appearance to somehow manipulate a man may work in the short term; however, Peter is pushing for a permanent change of a husband's heart.

Obviously, if the marriage is at stake—and, more to the point, if a husband's relationship with Jesus is at stake—how good a wife looks isn't top priority. It's not what matters when your marriage is in trouble. Some women think, *If I can only look as good as a younger woman or like the women at the office, maybe I could save my marriage.* Let me ask you a question: What happens to your man when you can't count on your looks to keep him in love with you and with the Lord?

No wonder Peter directs women to focus on their inner beauty rather than their outer looks.

What's more, in Peter's day the women were preoccupied with physical beauty. Lollia Paullina, the third wife of Emperor Caligula, purchased a dress valued at well over one million dollars. Women braided their hair with jeweled tortoise shells, ivory, and gold. They spent hours doing their hair! Not much has changed. But let me repeat, when a marriage is in trouble, beauty is not the issue.

What, then, is the fundamental problem?

It is a man's relationship with Jesus. That's always the heart of the problem. Let's make sure we don't lose sight of this main concern.

Furthermore, many wives in a troubled marriage pray for God to change the heart of their husband. Or, they pray that their husband recommits himself to their marriage.

Peter would say, "Try this. Pray that God changes you so that as your husband is watching, he sees that God has hold of your heart. Pray that Jesus in you is so attractive that your husband will want what you have." That is what will make a difference.

3. The Block of Attitude

Peter suggests that the building block of attitude is also critical. He writes,

> Instead, it should be that of your inner self, the unfading beauty of a gentle and quiet spirit, which is of great worth in God's sight. For this is the way the holy women of the past who put their hope in God used to make themselves beautiful. They were submissive to their own husbands, like Sarah, who obeyed Abraham and called him her master. You are her daughters if you do what is right and do not give way to fear.
>
> 1 PETER 3:4–6

I realize that on the surface Peter's advice in this section may be disheartening for some wives. He says that God asks wives to show a "gentle and quiet spirit." Some women may protest, "Well, I do talk. I'm loud. I like to talk, and I talk a lot. That's what my husband tells me." We need to be careful not to misunderstand this. Peter is not saying that wives have to be quiet and never talk.

The word for *quiet* used here is a specific word that denotes tranquility, referring to inner peace. Peter is saying that it is possible to have peace within yourself, even be at ease, when you are in a turbulent marriage.

How about when you are in a "spiritually mismatched marriage"? Inner peace is trusting that there is a God who can still do what you can't do. This peace flows from the confidence you have in God to transform your relationship.

Personally speaking, when our son was going through a spiritual rebellion, I wanted more than anything to change him. I devised many plans that were aimed at changing my son. As I have aged, I have realized that I do not have the power to do that. God does. I cannot change anybody.

Not my son. Not my daughter. Not my wife.

My role is to believe that God is a great big God who can do the work that I cannot do. I am convinced more than ever that when our spouse is not where God wants him or her to be, we need to say, "God, change my attitude; help me to grow in my relationship with You."

For us visual types, Peter paints a picture. He says to be "like Sarah." Genesis, chapter 18, records her amazing story for us. Here, the angel of the Lord came and announced to Abraham, "Sarah your wife will have a son" (v. 10). For her part, Sarah was in the tent listening. When she heard this amazing announcement, she actually laughed. She couldn't believe that God was able to open her womb again. Sarah said: "After I have become old, shall I have pleasure, my lord being old also?" (v. 12 NASB). Apparently, Sarah assessed the status of her life at that point and concluded, "We're washed up."

What advice does God give this woman who feels all washed up? The angel of the Lord then came to Sarah and raised this question, "Is anything too difficult for the LORD?" (v. 14 NASB). That is the question! When you are in a marriage that is not working, or when you have a husband who is being disobedient, that is always the question: Is anything too difficult for the Lord?

A MODERN DAY "SARAH"

Although Sarah had her doubts and her insecurities, ultimately she had the conviction to believe there is a God in heaven who can do the impossible. What about you? How big is your God? Are you willing to trust His blueprint for your marriage makeover? Regardless of how you answer those questions, I know God can do the impossible because of what He did for Dan and Linda—which leads me to one of my favorite stories. This is a remarkable couple who attended the church where I served as pastor. I've had the privilege of watching them walk from brokenness to wholeness. See if Linda's testimony melts away some of the disbelief you may have that God still radically transforms marriages in crisis.

Here's their story as told by Linda:

After five years of marriage, our relationship was becoming strained. We were growing emotionally and physically distant. Dan's job required him to travel overseas for weeks at a time, which only increased the distance between us. During the Christmas season of 1995, I told Dan that if he was not able to change the choices he was making in his life, he would need to leave our home. Unwilling to change, we began what would be a three-year separation.

My first reaction was, "There must be a way to fix this." I immediately looked for counselors to help us. I wanted to engage Dan to talk about our marriage and, frankly, I tried to force progress. However, it didn't take me too long to realize that God needed to be in control, not me. As with Sarah, I could see that even my situation was not too difficult for the Lord to heal. So, what did I do?

95

First, my reliance was placed on the Lord. He sustained me. I truly believe that at our deepest hour of need, there is only one place for us to turn: the loving arms of God with full trust and dependence on Him. Regardless of what Dan did, or the eventual outcome of the marriage, God was very clear that I needed to be healthy—spiritually and emotionally. He granted me the strength to live my life, day to day, working full-time and being a mom to Alex, who was two at the time. God filled me up in different ways. I would sing myself to sleep at night using praise song sheets that were printed in the Sunday bulletin. This helped to pull in the peace of God to fend off nightmares.

Pause with me for a moment. What do you fill your spirit with as you drift off to sleep? Is it the drone of late-night television with its caustic fare? Perhaps a Harlequin romance novel or a movie that spikes your longing for something other than what you have? Let's not race by the power of Linda's simple decision to meditate on songs with biblical themes. You, like Linda, can experience a more peaceful rest when you choose wisely what you allow into your mind, especially late at night. She continued:

This season of separation was also the first time in my life that I literally got down on my knees at my bedside and prayed. God granted me peace in a difficult situation, specifically the times when I could tell that Satan was trying to find opportunities to pull me, and our marriage, down. I remember many times saying aloud, "Get behind me Satan, you shall not prevail—not in my life and not in my marriage!" I also repeated the verse, "Be still, and know that I am God" (Psalm 46:10). When I would get anxious or have doubts, that verse was very calming for me.

God also prompted me to surround myself with people who would influence me positively and to be God-centered rather than me-focused. I joined a family Bible study through church, where my son, Alex, could attend with me. That was a stabilizing, consistent opportunity for me to nurture my faith and have ongoing prayer support.

God also granted me a heart of grace. I did not become embittered toward Dan. This attitude served to be a witness to many people in my life who could not understand it but could see that it was God's unconditional love shining through me. I maintained my integrity and privacy about our marriage. I did not go out and speak ill of Dan to other people.

You may recall our discussion in the previous chapter about keeping "your stuff" private. Remember rule #5? It said, "I will work out my conflict with my spouse, not my friends." Linda wisely knew that bad-mouthing her husband only served to poison the waters that others drink. She continued:

I also tried very hard not to lecture Dan. He needed to come to terms with God, and I was not to play a role in making that happen. Friends and family would ask me, particularly after several years, "How long are you going to wait?" I reminded them that I was waiting on God, who does not have a time clock. What others saw was a hopeless situation; I had faith that God was capable to heal no matter how long it took.

Every day I was convinced that marriage is for a lifetime; it is not a commitment that I only keep when it feels good or when I am happy. God did not promise me happiness. He promised me peace in Him under any circumstances. And while I also learned that love is not a feeling, it's a choice, I was terribly sad for Dan during this time. I knew what I was seeing in him and hearing from him was not the man I married, nor was it the man God intended him to be.

As I grew closer to God, I watched Dan running further from Him. I was completely helpless and had no control over that. However, I could pray and read Scripture to continue to affirm my own beliefs on marriage that, in turn, enabled me to grow in my own spiritual health.

As for the element of adornment, I did not set out to make over my physical appearance in any way to "win him back." Dan and I were far beyond that. In retrospect, Dan has commented that he could see the changes inside of me: my peace of mind, my inner strength, and my relationship with Christ. So, he could see what God was establishing inside of me.

Do you see the wisdom Linda exercised here? Had she tried to manipulate Dan or compete for his attention using her physical appearance, it would be like reaching over and yanking the wheel from the hands of God because she either didn't or couldn't trust God to steer their relationship back onto the right path. Instead, Linda basically told the Lord she'd leave the driving to Him. Which was, given the bumps ahead in their relationship, an incredibly prudent decision. She said:

> In spite of my efforts, Dan wanted me to let go of the marriage. Even when I agreed, God was not done with Dan's heart. This might surprise some people: I am the one who initiated divorce proceedings, not because I wanted the divorce but something

led me to do it. I wonder if it was God's hand so that Dan would finally be forced to face a decision. I was honestly at a point that I was ready for whatever was to come. I had grieved the loss of my marriage. I had accepted that no matter what happened, God was my Savior and He would not let go of me.

And I knew He had not let go of Dan either.

By the summer of 1998, we had gone through divorce mediation. We had all of the papers drawn up and the decisions finalized. We had even gone through what is called "marriage closure therapy." I was at peace with God. I was waiting for Dan and his lawyer to finish their signatures.

Unbeknownst to me, Dan was still wrestling with God, and God in His grace was not allowing Dan to take the final step in our divorce. Dan came to a point that summer when he no longer could cope with the sinfulness, the emptiness, and the loneliness of his life circumstance. He now says, "I knew that I needed to come back to God, and in order to do that, I needed to come back to Linda."

When, at the eleventh hour, Dan humbly called and asked if I would even consider reconciliation, my first thought was, *Of course I'll consider this, it is what I have been praying for three years.* My heart was grateful that Dan was finally submitting his will to God. I was as relieved for him in that moment as I was for our marriage.

Neither of us had a clue how we were going to rebuild this marriage that had been all but legally written off. I just kept trusting God to lead us. He knew how to bridge the gap between spending time together and actually repairing our marriage. God's plan for us was to attend a weekend marriage workshop. A friend had given me a brochure about this workshop two years prior. I had saved it all that time—just in case. Dan can attest that for me to be able to find a single piece of paper within even a week's time, amongst my many cluttered piles at home, is nothing short of a miracle. But God knew I would need that piece of paper someday! This ended up being the foundation we needed to start working together again.

By the way, if you and your spouse find yourself in need of either a complete marriage makeover or perhaps just a touch up, you'll find the Weekend to Remember® marriage getaway hosted by FamilyLife® to be life changing. More than 90,000 people a year attend one of the hundreds of weekend conferences held all across the country. For details, allow me to point you to their website, FamilyLife.com. That said, here's the rest of Linda's story.

Having attended the retreat, I had to decide what attitude I was going to take back into my marriage. With the heart of grace that God had blessed me with, I did not rehash the years of separation. I did not hang things over Dan's head out of bitterness. I did not play the martyr. And I never have. I did not even entertain that kind of attitude. Instead, I loved him, unconditionally. That is what God tasked me with when I agreed to marry Dan. What a blessing that God allowed us to move forward rather than waste our time reliving the past.

Certainly, a lot has happened over the last five years. At this point, we both can attest to the awesome ways our relationship has grown, and [it] is actually stronger [now] than prior to our separation. We both give the credit to God's sustaining grace and love. We were blessed with the addition of Sydney to our family three years ago, and . . . since that time [we've] had our third child. A family that neither of us thought we'd have is now a living testament to how God can repair a broken marriage and bless it fully.

Talk about proof that God will use the action, adornment, and attitude blocks to remake your marriage!

BUILDING BLOCKS FOR MEN ONLY

Now, let's shift gears and examine the two building blocks Peter provides the men to build up their relationship with their wives: the "understanding" and the "honor blocks." Both can be found in 1 Peter 3:7. As we work through these, remember to ponder, What would Jesus do if He faced what I face in my relationship?

1. The Block of Understanding

Peter begins by challenging husbands to live with their wives in an understanding way. The original language says, "according to knowledge." The clear implication of this command is that Peter knows we men tend not to understand our wives. We may think we know what they need, but too often we miss the mark.

What's the big deal, you say?

Allow me to illustrate how serious this concern really is. Imagine a woman going to her favorite restaurant for lunch. Let's say she's not starving and, in fact, she's concerned about watching her diet. Scanning the menu, she finds just the ticket: a fruit salad, a small roll, and perhaps a glass of unsweetened iced tea. As she closes the menu, she starts to picture a dress she's always wanted to buy—if only she could lose that extra five pounds.

The waiter appears table side. He takes her order, smiles, and then ten minutes later returns with a 16-ounce porterhouse steak, mashed garlic potatoes smothered in thick gravy, and batter-dipped onion rings with a tall beer. At that point, the conversation might go something like this:

"Sir, there's been a mistake." She shifts in her seat.

"Really?" He looks at the order ticket. "No mistake."

She shakes her head, trying to be pleasant. "Yes, actually there is. I believe I ordered the fruit plate and unsweetened tea."

He nods. "You did indeed." He proceeds to set the porterhouse, potatoes, rings and beer in front of her. "You want some rolls and butter?"

Now she's steaming. There isn't a language barrier. The waiter isn't new. She crosses her arms and raises her voice. "Excuse me, if you know that I ordered a fruit plate, why did you bring me a steak?"

He considers that for a moment. "Because, if I were having lunch, I can't imagine eating something so light, especially not a salad. I'd want some red meat."

And so it is. If we say we want to meet the needs of our wives but then treat them the way we like to be treated, guess what? Using this analogy, they'll leave the table hungry, confused, and upset with the service. If that happens over time, can you blame them for thinking about switching restaurants?

Of course, the disconnect runs deep within us guys. We, like the waiter, even after being confronted with the fact that the customer is not happy, cannot fathom why anyone would want to be served the fruit plate. There are at least five areas where we men typically fail to fully understand our wives:

We don't understand their love needs.

We don't understand how they think.

We don't understand how to be a help to them.

We don't understand their emotions.

We don't understand their need for relationship.

Briefly, let's look at these five areas where we must gain a heart of understanding in order to be successful in our marriage.

We don't understand their love needs. Gary Chapman, the author of *The Five Love Languages*, has identified five ways that men and women express love: words of affirmation, gifts, service, time, and touch.[16] There are exceptions of course, but men primarily show their love through service or touch. According to FamilyLife's marriage specialist, Dennis Rainey, this is because men usually define romance with the word *sex* while women define romance with the word *relationship*. Indeed, women tend to show love through words of affirmation, gifts, and time. Both are part of God's design. They're just different forms of a couple's love language.

In our home, my love languages are time and touch while my wife's are words of affirmation and service. On a practical level, what that means is I can't get enough time alone with Joan because she is busily engaged in acts of service. And she doesn't hear words of affirmation often enough because I would rather show her my love through touch.

Here's the danger. If we fail to understand that we have fundamental differences in how we show love to each other, we will most likely conclude, wrongly, that our spouse does not love us. Why? He or she is not speaking our love language. Case in point.

Some time ago, I was counseling a doctor and his wife. I asked the woman, "How do you know that your husband loves you?" She didn't hesitate. She claimed that she couldn't see any evidence that he loved her. As she spoke, her highly educated husband gripped the chair so hard his knuckles turned white. He listened as long as he could until he could not take it anymore. He blurted out, "How can you say I don't love you? Why do you think I work eighty hours a week? I have given you a nice house, a nice car, and good food to eat. What more do you want from me?"

Obviously, the man's love language was service. He did love his wife, but she concluded by his actions that he was in love with his job since he never spent any time with her and rarely spoke any words of affirmation to her. Every hardworking male needs to read the counsel found in Proverbs that says, "A bowl of vegetables with someone you love is better than steak with someone you hate" (15:17 NLT).

Before we spend too much time providing steaks and cars and houses, Peter says, "Husbands . . . live with your wives in an understanding way" (1 Peter 3:7 NASB). If you are unsure what really communicates love to your wife, ask her.

We don't understand how they think. Author John Gray penned the best seller *Men Are from Mars, Women Are from Venus*. He identifies a second problem that men have in understanding their wives. We do not grasp how women think! Gray insists that women do their thinking in groups—which is consistent with their high need for relationships.[17] Have you ever watched two couples eating dinner at a restaurant? If one of the ladies needs to use the restroom, she invites the other woman to join her. That's the relationship aspect kicking in. I doubt you'll find a guy on a double date asking his male counterpart, "I'm going to the restroom, care to join me?"

Men, you see, take their restroom breaks alone.

Likewise, men conduct their serious thinking alone in a cave. They do not normally like to share their business with anyone. In fact, the bigger the problem, the farther into the cave he goes to sort out what needs to be done. Only when he has an answer will a man surface. By contrast, women are more likely to talk about their marital problems or family struggles with their friends.

So what? Here's where the difficulty surfaces. Far too many men disengage from conversation with their wives because (1) as a guy they don't feel the need for dialogue, (2) they may not be comfortable talking aloud until they've had a chance to process issues alone, (3) they may have nothing to say on a given subject, and (4) men are far less likely to see the need for marital or family counseling because they assume they can solve all their own problems.

To be successful living in an understanding way with your wife, start by refusing to discount her need for conversation. Resist the temptation to wave her off with a dismissive remark about how she talks too much. If you don't have a particular opinion about what's on her heart, just listen. Why not pray that you'll learn how to listen more attentively— even sacrificially when your bride demonstrates a need to talk. Believe it or not, six of the most romantic words a guy can speak are these: "This sounds interesting. Tell me more."

We don't understand how to be a help to them. Typically, when a man sees that his wife has a problem, his tendency is to offer a five- or six-step plan that will bring resolution to the problem. He's a fixer. Occasionally that's helpful, but more often than not his wife is not interested in the brilliant six-step plan. Sometimes she just wants to vent—no solutions, just a safe place where she can unload the burden she's been carrying around with her. For the most part, she wants her husband to listen to her, to give her a hug, and reassure her that everything will be okay.

Let me give you an example. My daughter, Michelle, got married during the summer of 2004. Prior to her wedding she spent four years overseas engaged in mission work. Naturally, she had developed some dear friendships there. She and her future husband, Paul, planned to return to the mission field, but it wouldn't be for at least a year.

Paul, sensing that his bride-to-be was deeply missing her friends, wrote Michelle before their wedding and said, "Words cannot express how I would like to support you as you grieve the loss of your friends. I wish I could be there, hold you, and assure you that we will be seeing all your friends again." Paul wisely met Michelle's need by empathizing with her—not sending her away on the next flight.

If we are to learn to live in an understanding way in terms of meeting our wife's needs, start by empathizing with her. Use phrases such as, "Boy, honey, that must have been hurtful to you," or "I can see how that would cause a real problem for your friendship with our neighbor," or "If I were in your shoes, I'd have the same reaction." If you sense that she really wants more than empathy, leave the list alone. Simply ask her: How can I help? How can I be a support to you?

We don't understand their emotions. In my early marital counseling experience, I failed miserably with highly emotional women. I am convinced that the advice that I gave them was sound. The problem was that I offered my solutions and I concluded that was all that I needed to do. I discovered, however, that *solutions are not much good until a husband or wife gets through the emotional pain.* In fact, the pain is far more likely to be the obstacle to victory than an ignorance of what the

Bible says we are supposed to do. It takes time to work through emotion. It isn't a logical process.

Here are some dos and don'ts as you seek to understand her emotions:

- DON'T TELL YOUR WIFE THAT SHE'S ACTING TOO EMOTIONAL OR BEING TOO SENSITIVE.

- DON'T BECOME IMPATIENT IF YOUR WIFE CAN'T EXPLAIN WHY SHE IS FEELING WHAT SHE DOES.

- DON'T JUDGE HER FEELINGS OR TELL HER SHE SHOULDN'T FEEL THE WAY SHE DOES.

- DO LISTEN AND PRAY FOR INCREASED SENSITIVITY TO HER HEART.

- DO TAKE YOUR TIME. GIVE HER A STRONG SHOULDER ON WHICH TO LEAN, CRY, LAUGH, AND LOVE.

- DO IMITATE HOW JESUS INTERACTED WITH WOMEN LIKE MARY AND MARTHA OR LIKE THE WOMAN WHO, TO THE SHOCK OF THE DISCIPLES, POURED ON JESUS' FEET A PERFUME THAT HAD THE VALUE OF ONE YEAR'S SALARY.

We don't understand their need for relationship. Normally a man finds his purpose, significance, and fulfillment in his job. When a man loses a job, it can be devastating to his self-image. Most women, however, find their sense of purpose and validation through the quality of their relationships. This is why a woman wants her husband to ask about her friends and why it's so important for her to see you engaged in a meaningful relationship with your own children.

Furthermore, your wife wants to know about the people at your work, but not because she doesn't trust you or is jealous of anyone there. Rather, she feels connected to you as a man when she learns about your world. This high need for relationship prompts her to desire to know what you feel about everything—life, work, family, and friends.

What happens when a man doesn't understand and doesn't attempt to meet her need for relationship? She can easily feel that he does not love her and, in time, she may conclude that she does not love him either. Take, for example, Kevin. As I got to know Kevin, I found him to be a dedicated husband. He truly loved his wife, Alison. Since his love language was service, he worked long hours to provide for Alison and his family. You might say he was the strong, silent type.

Unfortunately, one of his wife's primary love languages was words of affirmation. Kevin was not good with words. Alison was sensitive, caring, outgoing, and highly relational. As husband and wife, they were a wonderful complement to each other, but their differences in this area led Alison to wrongly conclude that Kevin did not love her.

At a vulnerable moment, a man at Alison's work expressed the words she always longed to hear from Kevin. This outsider even started writing her long love letters. These verbal expressions by the other man confused Alison and threatened her marriage with Kevin. It was obvious that the other man was speaking Alison's love language; Kevin needed to learn how to connect relationally with his wife, and to succeed, he had to learn how to speak her language.

In one of our first sessions, I told Kevin that he had to express his love for his wife in words, not just his acts of service. Since the other man was already writing long love letters, I suggested that Kevin try something different. I didn't know exactly what to recommend so I said, "God is the author of creation. Why don't you ask Him to reveal to you a way to express your love for your wife?"

A week or so later they came into my office again and I said, "Did God give you a way to verbally show your love for your wife?"

Kevin said, "Yes."

"What did you do?" I asked.

"God led me to write notes that I put on Alison's mirror in the master bathroom twice a day."

I then looked at Alison and asked, "How did you feel when you got these notes?" She started to cry and said the notes were great. I then asked if she had kept any of them. Still crying, she reached into her purse and pulled out a large stack of 3″x 5″ cards. She carried them with her wherever she went.

In one note, Kevin wrote, "You are my precious one and for that I am truly thankful to the Lord. I can't wait to grow deeper in our relationship with the Lord and together. Love, KC." In another note he wrote, "I just wanted to let you know that I really enjoy holding your hand as we drive. It communicates so much to me without saying anything. Love, KC." In yet another note he wrote, "Thanks for the love and patience that you have with the girls with their school work. I love your charm as a mother! Love, KC."

Kevin is a husband who proves that a man, even in a troubled marriage, can learn to do what Peter says in 1 Peter 3:7 and build on the block of understanding. There's also a second building block in this passage: the honor block. Peter writes, "and treat them with respect." The word *respect* translated is the same word that appears elsewhere in 1 Peter when Peter references "the precious blood of Jesus Christ." In other words, the way that you look at the precious blood of Jesus Christ is the way you ought to look at your wife.

2. The Block of Honor

That is compelling to me. Does my wife know that she is precious to me? Does yours? Peter contends that there are three reasons why you and I need to communicate to our wives that they are precious:

She is the weaker vessel.

She is an equal vessel.

And, so that our prayers will not be hindered.

Treat her as precious because she is the weaker vessel. What is that supposed to mean? Well, I think it simply means what it implies. Usually women are not as tall, they are not as heavy, and they are not as muscular as men are. We're talking about physical strength here. We have to be careful not to confuse weaker with less worthy or less valuable. The implication is that I can show my wife that she is precious if I gladly do those physical tasks that are harder for her to do: opening jars, lifting heavy objects, moving furniture, and hauling the little ones over my shoulder at bedtime.

Treat her as precious because she is an equal vessel. First Peter says our wives are "fellow heir[s] of the grace of life" (3:7 NASB). Just about the time we men might be sticking out our chest and feeling like we're something special—you know, the leader of the house—the Bible says in effect, "No, you're not more special. You are equal to your wife in what matters the most: you are equal in My eyes." Then comes the phrase that is rather poignant: "of the grace of life."

What does that mean—practically speaking?

If my wife is acting inappropriately—say, she's being rude, unthankful, or inconsiderate—what should I do? I am to treat her like a fellow heir of the grace of life; I need to show her kindness and forgiveness because she is a child of God. Even if she is not meeting my needs or is having one of "those moments," or is not responding the way I want her to respond, my wife needs God's love just as I do. I demonstrate that she truly is precious to me when I extend a Christlike attitude toward her as often as is needed.

Treat her as precious so that our prayers will not be hindered. Over the years, I have counseled so many couples who have said, "I don't know why our marriage is in the trouble that it's in because we pray. We pray constantly and yet our prayers don't seem to make any difference." The 1 Peter 3:7 passage tells us why our prayers may not be making any difference. We can pray about our marriage, but if we are not demonstrating that our wife is precious to us, Peter says there is an inevitable result: your prayers will be hindered. Did you know that?

You might even be praying daily for your marriage, hoping somehow that your wife will change. However, because you are not treating her as precious, because you are not attempting to really understand her needs, and because you don't make time to engage her in real relationship, you're kinking the hose. Those prayers that could help so much are rendered ineffective. God is not even going to hear your prayers!

What are you and I supposed to do? This passage emphasizes that we need to follow in Jesus' steps. We men must pray, "God help me to be the kind of man you want me to be. I pray that my wife may see, through my behavior, my love for Jesus. And I pray that through my actions, my wife will see that she is precious to me!"

A FINAL THOUGHT

If you are a woman following Peter's blueprint for a marriage makeover by using the building blocks of action, adornment, and attitude, or if you are a man and are laying a foundation with the blocks of understanding and honor, remember this: Jesus is the mortar that holds your home together. This is not some human enterprise that can be snapped together like a Lego set and then be expected to withstand the storms of life.

You need Jesus, who walked on this earth and who understands human temptations, to finish the good things He has begun to do in your heart. He alone can give you the wisdom and strength to rebuild your marriage. Best of all, He desires and freely offers to supply you with all of the patience and insight needed in your marriage. That's especially good news since we are about to learn something amazing in the next chapter about the role of romance.

THE ONE THING

This week reread the portion of the chapter that is most appropriate to your situation as a husband or a wife. Then, as a place to start, consider which building block you will ask the Lord to help you apply in your marriage.

CHAPTER 7

ROMANCE BY THE BOOK

I know what you might be thinking.

Romance? George, are you crazy? We're sleeping in separate rooms! I'd rather walk across hot coals than pursue romance with that thoughtless, insensitive ingrate. I can appreciate your feelings. But, remember, we are praying for God to work a miracle in your marriage. While romance may be the last thing on your mind today, let's not lose sight of the big picture.

Think about the stories of John and Amy, Grant and Penny, and Mark and Missy in chapter one. Each of these couples were headed for a divorce after an affair had rocked their marriages. But God gave them His power to hope, to forgive, and to love each other again. I firmly believe that one day by His grace, you, too, will find pleasure and warmth in the company of your spouse.

Now if your marriage is in trouble because your husband or wife has had an affair, I realize you might have severe reservations at the prospect of a future romance together. You're wondering, *How can I possibly give myself away in this most intimate of human expressions and trust myself to the arms of that monster! I cringe whenever he or she walks into the room. I don't want to be touched or kissed, and I certainly can't imagine being sexually intimate.*

Let me be clear. I'm not suggesting that you throw caution to the wind and fake a romantic interest in your spouse if there are broken wedding vows. You feel violated. Trust has been breached. When your spouse has had an affair, there's a pain you feel that is in some ways worse than if your spouse had died. Why? Had your spouse died from an accident or an illness, you would grieve, but you wouldn't feel betrayed.

Further complicating your feelings, you may be plagued with a host of unsettling questions, such as: "What's wrong with me? Couldn't I provide the sex, the comfort, the companionship that my spouse wanted? Why was it sought someplace else?" Or, you may be feeling intense anger: "How could he or she do this to me? To us? To our kids?" This is understandable.

That said, the challenge you now face is twofold: seeking forgiveness and rebuilding trust. Only after these two things have happened can romance be rekindled. Much of what we've covered in prior chapters has dealt with the need to seek forgiveness and healing. So, before giving you a Bible-based perspective on romance, a few thoughts about rebuilding trust with your mate are in order.

It is unrealistic for me to say, "I want you to trust your spouse right now"—as if you can just wave a magic wand and the pain and distrust will be erased. Why? Because trust is never granted in a moment. Look at it this way. You wouldn't have a stranger on the street babysit your kids, would you? Why not? Because you can't trust a stranger—you don't know her. You'd have to watch someone in action over time before you could trust that person with your precious ones.

Trust is something that all of us must earn.

When a spouse has an affair, trust vanishes.

Like a bank account or "trust fund," your mate has drained the account and you're overdrawn. Trust is not going to be recaptured in a moment. Many trust-earning "deposits" must be made into your mutual account before the sense of security is restored. So, part of the process of restoration is finding a number of shared experiences where trust can be rehabilitated.

For example: A wife might say, "I trust that you're going to come home at night when you say you'll be home and that you're not going to be with that other woman." Each time he is faithful to the agreed upon timetable, a deposit is made into your mutual trust fund. Likewise, as he makes himself accountable to you and his accountability partner, additional deposits are made.

In time, you will begin to experience trust again because his actions demonstrate that he is trustworthy. At that point, you as a couple are in the best position to rediscover what romantic love is all about. That said, consider what I'm about to share as a foundation for your future romance as God heals your marriage.

A LOVE LIKE NO OTHER

Even in the healthiest of marriages, most couples go through a period when the flames of romance flicker. We don't intend for that to happen. When we say "I do" at the altar, it's our expectation that this man or woman of our dreams is going to continue to fulfill our life forever, but sometimes the warmth and the passion we felt at the altar diminishes as time goes by.

That reality was captured in an article I came across some time ago, entitled, "Seven Stages of a Marriage Cold."[18] Maybe you can identify with this. The following is the attitude that a husband has toward his wife's cold through the first seven years of their marriage:

First year: Husband says to his wife, who has a bad cold, "Sugar dumpling, I'm worried about my baby girl. You've got a bad sniffle. I'm putting you in the hospital for a general checkup and a good rest. I know the food's lousy, but I'll bring your meals in from Rossini's. I already have it arranged."

Second year: "Listen darling, I don't like the sound of your cough. I called Dr. Miller to rush over here. Now you go to bed like a good girl just for your dear old papa."

Third year: "Honey, maybe you better lie down. Nothing like a little rest when you feel punk. I'll bring you something to eat. Do we have any soup in the house?"

Fourth year: "Look dear, be sensible. After you feed the kids and get the dishes washed, maybe you'd better hit the sack for awhile."

Fifth year: "Why don't you get up, get yourself an aspirin, and stop complaining so much."

Sixth year: "If you'd just gargle or something instead of sitting around and barking in my face like a seal, I'd appreciate it."

Seventh year: "For Pete's sake, stop sneezing. What are you trying to do, give me pneumonia or something?"

What is true of the "marriage cold" is often true of many other aspects of our relationship with our spouse. We start strong and then something happens. This phenomenon begs the question, Why does the honeymoon end? The answer to this question—as well as the remedy to stave off the seemingly inescapable reality—can be found in the Song of Solomon. This Old Testament book is not familiar to many of us because, quite frankly, it is a difficult book to read.

The difficulty is that it's unlike any other book of the Bible. This is a play presented through poetry. The book is a script with the lines of the various actors. The margin of your Bible may identify who is giving the line, but some Bibles don't, so we just have to guess. In the Hebrew Bible (that's the language that the first half of the Bible was originally written in), this is not an issue because there are feminine endings and masculine endings on verbs and nouns, so it is always easy to tell who is talking.

There are two principle characters in the Song of Solomon: King Solomon and his Shulammite bride. As the play unfolds, we get a taste of their courtship, their marriage, their honeymoon, and the inevitable conflict that married couples face. In chapter 1, verse 2, we learn what the Shulammite thinks about her fiancé: "Let him kiss me with the kisses of his mouth—for your love is more delightful than wine." What is she saying about this guy she's dating?

He's a great kisser.

In addition, apparently, he has fresh breath—two good dating tips for all men. This bride-to-be says, "Pleasing is the fragrance of your perfumes" (v. 3). Solomon is smart enough to put on some deodorant. He smells good and, she adds, "Your name is like perfume poured out." He has a great reputation, so in summary she concludes, "No wonder the maidens love you!"

Do you see what's happening here? While they are dating, she observes that Solomon is not only a great kisser, he's got fresh breath, he smells good, he's got a great reputation, all the other girls say he's hot, and guess what? She's astounded that this incredible man is all hers. We can understand why she is so impressed that someone this amazing would take notice of her when we see how she views herself.

In verse 5, she says, "Dark am I, yet lovely, O daughters of Jerusalem." The Shulammite recognizes that there's an attractiveness about her, but her insecurity shows: "Do not stare at me because I am dark, because I am darkened by the sun" (v. 6). Unlike today where getting a golden tan is job one in the summer, she's a bit self-conscious about the color of her skin. Continuing on, she explains, "My mother's sons were angry with me and made me take care of the vineyards; my own vineyard I have neglected." She's saying that because her brothers made her work in their vineyards, she could not give attention to herself the way she would have liked.

Her predicament sort of reminds me of the movie *Ever After*, where Drew Barrymore plays the part of Cinderella. In a number of scenes she's dressed in common farm clothes digging in the dirt when her prince arrives. She's dirty and a little smelly. When the dashing prince stopped by, she was not ready for him. That's the picture here. Likewise, the Shulammite is saying, "Do not look at me, because I do not feel good about the way I look."

I find it interesting that this girl, while self-conscious about her appearance, still bubbles over with praise for her husband-to-be. Using poetic language, she says,

> Like an apple tree among the trees of the forest
>> is my lover among the young men.
>> I delight to sit in his shade,
>> and his fruit is sweet to my taste.

He has taken me to the banquet hall,
and his banner over me is love.

SONG OF SOLOMON 2:3–4

Let's put this in contemporary terms.

The picture here is of a lover (Solomon) who rents a plane and flies it with a banner in tow that broadcasts to the whole world: I love the Shulammite! This story is really a 900 BC Cinderella tale where the farm girl meets the prince; the prince falls madly in love with the farm girl and, in turn, sweeps her off her feet. This prince, this wonderful man who smells good, who looks good, who has a great reputation, who's hot, whose banner announces his love, can't live without her love.

Now isn't that what leads us to the altar?

We are excited about the wonderful person God has brought into our lives. So, with heartfelt passion, we recite our vows to one another, which is exactly what happens next in the story. We find Solomon speaking to his bride on their wedding day. He says,

How beautiful you are, my darling!
Oh, how beautiful!
Your eyes behind your veil are doves.
Your hair is like a flock of goats
descending from Mount Gilead.

Your teeth are like a flock of sheep just shorn,
coming up from the washing.
Each has its twin;
not one of them is alone.

Your lips are like a scarlet ribbon;
your mouth is lovely.

> Your temples behind your veil
> are like the halves of a pomegranate.
>
> SONG OF SOLOMON 4:1–3

Most wives today would probably ask for some I.D. if their husband spoke like this! But understand that Solomon is expressing his heartfelt appreciation for his Shulammite bride on their wedding day in the poetic vernacular of the time. Having publicly celebrated their marriage, it's off to the honeymoon. Solomon as the happy bridegroom says,

> I have come into my garden, my sister, my bride;
> I have gathered my myrrh with my spice.
> I have eaten my honeycomb and my honey;
> I have drunk my wine and my milk.
>
> SONG OF SOLOMON 5:1

Then someone off stage says, "Eat, O friends, and drink; drink your fill, O lovers" (5:1). Solomon and his bride consummate their marriage in style. Just as it is for all who marry, there comes a time when the honeymoon period is over. We pick up with the Shulammite bride speaking:

> I slept but my heart was awake.
> Listen! My lover is knocking:
> "Open to me, my sister, my darling,
> my dove, my flawless one."
>
> SONG OF SOLOMON 5:2

She, for whatever reason, was not interested so she starts making excuses to avoid intimacy. She says, "I have taken off my robe—must I put it on again? I have washed my feet—must I soil them again?" (5:3). Solomon, the king, comes to the queen's bedchambers. He knocks on the door and says in effect, "Sweetheart, flawless one, I want to be with you tonight." Notice her response: "Solomon, I've taken off my dress, how can I put it on? I have just washed my feet. You expect me to get my feet dirty again? Thanks, but no thanks."

Put yourself in Solomon's place because all of us have experienced this at one time or another. We have come to someone we love to spend time with. We want to be with them. We have the purest of motives. We knock on the door, but the door remains shut and we hear a voice saying, "No thanks. I'm not interested right now."

What is the natural, human tendency when facing that kind of rejection? What races through our heads, naturally, are our rights and our needs. We immediately think selfishly . . . something along the lines of this: *I just give and give and give and I get nothing back. What's the deal? It's not right. I deserve better. If they're going to act that way, fine. I'm outta here.*

If anybody had a reason to feel that way, it would be Solomon.

He was the king. There was no one more powerful in all Palestine than Solomon. By what right could this woman deny him anything that he wanted? He could have easily demanded his rights. But he didn't. I want you to see something that is absolutely amazing. This disinterested bride was in for a surprise. She says,

My lover thrust his hand through the
    latch-opening;
    my heart began to pound for him.

I arose to open for my lover,
    and my hands dripped with myrrh,
    my fingers with flowing myrrh,
    on the handles of the lock.

SONG OF SOLOMON 5:4–5

121

You may think, What's this rascal up to? Is this a prank? Why is Solomon smearing something on the door? Here's what's going on. Having been rejected by his wife, Solomon leaves a bag of myrrh—a sweet perfume—on the door handle and, with it, the implicit message: Sweetheart, it's okay. I understand and I want you to know with this gift of love how much you mean to me.

Put yourself in the Shulammite bride's place. On the occasions when your spouse may have wanted to spend time with you or be intimate sexually and yet you said, "No, not tonight," what would your reaction be if your mate did what Solomon did in return for your rejection? Think about it. We reject and our spouse who, in turn, leaves us a bottle of our favorite perfume or a dozen red roses just to let us know how much he or she cares.

What would most wives do in a reasonably healthy marriage? I have asked this question of women around the world and the answer is always the same: You'd get up and go looking for him. You'd want to be with someone who loves you that much. That is precisely what this Shulammite bride does. She gets up and she starts looking through the streets for Solomon because she wants to be with this man who has demonstrated that kind of selfless love to her.

You see, Solomon has just done something absolutely selfless. He wasn't thinking about what was rightfully his. He was thinking about his wife and demonstrated that love and thoughtfulness in one of the most obvious ways any man could. As marriage expert Dennis Rainey points out, sacrifice is the language of romance. By sacrificing his agenda and his needs, Solomon's actions breathed romance into his relationship.

THE PLOT THICKENS

As the story unfolds, Solomon and the Shulammite bride meet. I can imagine what kind of meeting this was going to be. For his part, Solomon could have reminded her of the poor way she had treated him—especially so soon after their honeymoon. For her part, she could have taken out her black book and ticked off a list of times when she felt that Solomon wasn't doing all that he should have done in their relationship.

You see, it's natural to want to defend ourselves when we've been wronged. It's far too easy to go on the attack and remind our spouse of faults and shortcomings. It's also likely that this rift might have prompted the Shulammite to fret over the security she once enjoyed in their relationship. She might wonder, *Does he still love me? Does my prince really care for me? Is he still interested in this dark, comely woman whose vineyard is not always what it should be? Is he going to reject me now?*

Before she has a chance to say a word, Solomon speaks. Notice how he handles things:

You are beautiful, my darling, as Tirzah,
> lovely as Jerusalem,
> majestic as troops with banners.

Turn your eyes from me;
> they overwhelm me.
> Your hair is like a flock of goats
> descending from Gilead.

Your teeth are like a flock of sheep
> coming up from their washing.
> Each has its twin,
> not one of them is alone.

Your temples behind your veil
are like the halves of a pomegranate.

SONG OF SOLOMON 6:4–7

Sound familiar?

It should. This language may not mean much to us because it is not the kind of vows or words we would use on our wedding day. But Solomon is repeating his wedding vows. He spoke these same words to her on the day they were married. In effect, Solomon is saying, "Sweetheart, before you say one word, I want you to know something. I want you to know I love you every bit as much today—this day you rejected me—as I did the day you married me."

Think about it. Instead of pointing out your failures, what if your spouse left you a gift. Then later in a meeting that could have been very awkward, he or she says, "Sweetheart, don't say anything. I want you to know this. I love you every bit as much today as the day I married you." How are you going to react to that?

Probably the way this Shulammite bride reacts. She says, "I belong to my lover and his desire is for me" (7:10). Do you think she had evidence of that? Do you think by this point in their marriage, she could prove to the maidens that Solomon had an incredible, selfless desire for her? You bet she could! She thought she knew something about love when they were dating. She knew that her fiancé was pretty incredible. She knew that he did some wonderful things for her, but she did not learn about love until she married him.

That is the story of this book.

Interestingly, during the Middle Ages interpreters allegorized this book. Solomon was cast as a type of Christ in the Old Testament (that's the collection of books written before Jesus was born), and scholars in the Middle Ages said that this book was about the love of Jesus for the church rather than between a husband and wife. While there's no question that this is a love story between Solomon and his wife, it's easy to think it's analogous to Jesus and the church because, like the Shulammite bride, we fail to show Jesus the love that He shows us; and yet, Jesus does just what Solomon did. He continues to bring the gifts of perfume to anoint us and give fragrance to our stinking lives. He continues to let us know that He loves us every bit as much today as the day that He claimed us at Calvary—and He's going to keep on loving us that way—no matter what!

Why, then, does the honeymoon end?

The honeymoon ends because we stop loving like Jesus.

You might want to read that again.

The honeymoon ends because we get caught up in the pettiness of what's mine. We fail to see how sacrifice is the language of romance. We become far more concerned about our spouse doing his or her part than we dare ask of ourselves, *What would Jesus do in my situation?* Perhaps if we could learn to love our spouses like Solomon loved the Shulammite in these scenes, the honeymoon would never end.

THE ONE THING

Two of the best resources available to couples regarding romance in marriage is *Rekindling the Romance* by Dennis and Barbara Rainey, and License 4 Creative Intimacy—a collection of mystery dates for couples to take turns initiating. Order a copy from FamilyLife.com and pray that the Lord uses these tools to help you reignite your romance.

CHAPTER 8

SEEING IS BELIEVING

Earlier I shared with you the three questions I ask every couple that comes to me for marriage help. They are worth repeating—and, perhaps, committing to memory. As I've said, my experience tells me that an amazing 90 percent of the couples in troubled marriages who agree to these statements ultimately find and enjoy new life for their marriages.

How will you answer my three key questions:

1. DO YOU BELIEVE THAT THERE IS A GOD?
2. ARE YOU WILLING TO APPLY THE PRINCIPLES OF THE BIBLE TO YOUR LIFE?
3. WILL YOU PRAY FOR THE SPIRIT OF GOD TO STRENGTHEN YOU AND YOUR SPOUSE?

I also mentioned that for about 10 percent of the couples I work with, their marriage ends in divorce. That troubles me. Why? Because there is virtually no reason that these relationships had to fail, just as divorce is not the inevitable outcome for you. God didn't suddenly renege on His offer to share His riches, power, strength, and might with those in a needy marriage. Nor did He lose interest in mending broken lives.

Why, then, didn't that minority of couples experience healing? I'd say the primary reasons were:

- A REFUSAL TO APOLOGIZE, SEEK FORGIVENESS, AND START IN A NEW DIRECTION WHEN GOD PUTS HIS FINGER ON SOME ASPECT OF THE RELATIONSHIP THAT NEEDED WORK
- A FAILURE TO FOLLOW THROUGH ON COMPLETING THEIR HOMEWORK (I.E., DOING "THE ONE THING")
- AN UNWILLINGNESS TO CONTINUE TO PRAY THAT GOD WOULD BLESS AND HEAL THEIR MARRIAGE

I know God is still at work because I've witnessed the miraculous time and time again, not just in our church, but wherever I've taught the principles of this book—even in other countries. This approach is not some kind of snake oil peddled by George Kenworthy. Rather, it's straight from the heart of the Bible. Either we can trust God when He makes a promise, or we can't. I believe we can.

Consider the following powerful story of Nikkos and Kayla from a church in Lima, Peru. Their testimony demonstrates the power of the hand of God to rescue and sustain a marriage, even in the face of death. Nikkos was a lawyer; Kayla worked in a gas station. Much like the *Romeo and Juliet* story where the families opposed the relationship, Nikkos and Kayla married against the advice of their friends and families. Kayla's mother was a Christian who objected to Nikkos because he was not a Christian—never mind the fact that neither was Kayla.

Many of Nikkos's friends likewise objected to the marriage because they viewed Kayla as emotionally unstable and controlling. Nikkos's mother was unenthusiastic because Nikkos supported her and his little sister financially and she was afraid of losing that help.

Incidentally, in my counseling I've found that far too many couples never really weighed the differences in their family backgrounds and the potential consequences of those differences before they married. Then, years into married life, those deep-rooted influences often created conflicts that had to be worked out.

Let me suggest that you and your spouse go on a communication date and use the Family Background Discussion Sheet (Appendix B) as a tool to work through your individual histories. Doing so will help you see how your past may be affecting your relationship today—that's something Nikkos and Kayla desperately needed.

Not surprisingly, their marriage was rocky. Kayla was emotionally volatile, possessive, and controlling of Nikkos in many ways. But most of the serious problems revolved around two things: Nikkos's random disappearances and his relationship with his mother.

Nikkos had a habit of going out drinking with friends or even alone; when he did, he'd disappear for several days at a time. Neither his friends nor Kayla would know where he had gone, but when he reappeared he was almost always broke and, at least several times, displayed evidence that he had been with women—lipstick on the collar, perfume on his shirt, etc. When questioned, Nikkos said he was unable to remember what had happened.

The second source of constant tension was his failure, as the Bible teaches, to "leave and cleave." He needed to leave his mother's home and cleave (become one) to his wife (Genesis 2:24). For years, Nikkos continued to support his mother and little sister economically. Kayla didn't object to the support itself, but to the fact that Nikkos used money that was needed for paying bills or credit card debt to buy something nonessential like a new purse for his mother. Worse, Nikkos's mother demanded relatively frivolous things from him, and he found it impossible to say no.

Nikkos and Kayla both became Christians and attended church regularly. Although they grew as Christians somewhat, Nikkos struggled breaking ties with his mother and would still disappear occasionally with no explanation. As Kayla grew in the Lord, she became increasingly impatient with Nikkos's inconsistency and slow growth as a believer. They reached a crisis in their marriage and Nikkos suggested that they separate. Kayla agreed. By this time, they had a daughter.

Meanwhile, Nikkos began to struggle with his health. He suffered frequent fevers, weight loss, and respiratory problems. Eventually he was diagnosed as having HIV, but by this time he was Stage III. The response of Nikkos and Kayla was not unexpected. Nikkos realized he had been wasting his life and was not taking God seriously. Kayla realized how much she still loved Nikkos and would not want to lose him.

Nevertheless, after the initial shock of discovering his AIDS, both were back struggling to tolerate each other. Kayla was totally fed up with Nikkos's inability to say no to his mother and also to continue at times to disappear—which was probably how he had become infected with HIV in the first place. Nikkos was also frustrated with Kayla's constant criticism of him, even though he felt he probably deserved it. He had concerns, as well, about Kayla's lack of control when disciplining their daughter.

They decided to separate for a second time. Although living apart, Nikkos and Kayla sought counseling at their church. Using the principles from this book, they were counseled to stay together because:

- GOD'S COMMAND REGARDING MARRIAGE IS THAT IT IS PERMANENT UNTIL DEATH (SEE MARK 10:5–9).

- OBEYING GOD'S INSTRUCTION IS THE BEST THING YOU CAN DO FOR YOUR OWN SAKE, FOR THE SAKE OF YOUR FAMILY, AND FOR THE WAY IT HONORS GOD. THIS MEANS THAT EVEN WHEN A MARRIAGE LOOKS HOPELESS AND PAINFUL, THE BEST THING THAT WE CAN DO IF WE WANT TO EXPERIENCE GOD'S GOODNESS IN OUR LIVES IS TO DO WHAT HE CLEARLY STATES IS HIS PLAN FOR US (SEE JOHN 15:10–11).

- GOD SAYS THAT "IN ALL THINGS [HE] WORKS FOR THE GOOD OF THOSE WHO LOVE HIM, WHO HAVE BEEN CALLED ACCORDING TO HIS PURPOSE[11] (ROMANS 8:28).

- THEY LEARNED AND STUDIED WHAT LOVE IS, USING INSIGHTS IN I CORINTHIANS, CHAPTER 13

At least once a week, one of the church leaders met with Nikkos and Kayla to listen, pray, study the Bible, and offer counsel. Kayla became more emotionally stable, less controlling, and began to accept Nikkos's suggestions regarding disciplining their daughter. She started to love him and admire the kind of man he was.

Nikkos began to grow more in his relationship to God and to Kayla. He said no to his mother with increasing frequency. His disappearances became more rare and shorter, and his prayers were often for Kayla and their daughter to continue growing as Christians even after his impending death. Where there had once been a shaky and immature marriage—rocked by two separations—a surprisingly mature and solid marriage emerged. At the time of his death, he and Kayla were united in their love for each other.

THE TEST OF TIME

Another way I am convinced that God is still in the business of saving and restoring marriages is that the healing isn't temporary. Any couple can fake a change for a season. But I've witnessed countless couples who came to God in their brokenness and who are now years—even decades—later still enjoying the fruits of wholeness.

Take, for example, the story of Ivan and Breanna. When their relationship was at its worst, Ivan was distant, depressed, and sullen. He had no desire to be near Breanna and made his displeasure with her constantly clear. For her part, Breanna cried a lot, and while Ivan felt sorry to see her so hurt, he wouldn't change his behavior nor would he give an explanation for the negative change that had come over him. Breanna describes that dark period in their marriage as follows:

> Ivan used to wave good-bye to me when he left the house, but as things deteriorated he stopped doing that and stared straight ahead. He wouldn't even look at me. Ivan didn't want me to do anything for him—not his laundry, not his meals, not even sex. Among the hurtful things he said, he claimed he didn't love me and didn't think he ever had. He also said that he married me only because it was the right thing to do—I had been pregnant at the time.
>
> Soon, it felt like I was always walking on eggshells whenever Ivan was around. I started to put the children before Ivan since he was uninterested in a relationship with me. As things got almost unbearable between us, Ivan moved downstairs and then to an extended-stay hotel. He didn't want to spend time with either of our families, preferring to be at work where his coworkers became his confidantes.

I remember at one point Ivan asked if I was praying that he would fall in love with me again. He said that if I was, he wanted me to stop because that was something between him and God.

Now, fast forward seven years after God healed their marriage. You wouldn't recognize this couple, nor would you have a clue that they had once teetered on the brink of a divorce after Breanna learned of Ivan's affair. Today, Ivan is open and friendly. He talks freely and laughs with his wife. And, he's become the spiritual leader in his home. Breanna described the dramatic changes in their relationship this way:

Ivan has become an amazing servant-leader in our home, serving our daughters and me constantly and in ways I never would have imagined. He tells me he loves me several times a day—and he ends every phone conversation with those precious words. He waves good-bye to me when one of us leaves the house and even gets up out of his recliner to do so.

We go for walks together whenever we can. We run errands together and watch "chick flicks" on a regular basis. We never did that before. I've learned to ask when he would like to discuss difficult issues instead of just saying, "We need to talk." He loves being home and makes the children and me feel so special.

A transformation like this can only be explained as the work of God's Holy Spirit. Maybe you've read this far and desire to experience the amazing change that couples such as Ivan and Breanna have enjoyed. However, it's possible that you are unsure of where you stand with God. You've heard me talk about asking God to bless your marriage, but perhaps you don't feel you have that kind of connection to Him.

If so, see if this final story helps you embrace God in your life in a new and personal way. After many years in a rocky marriage, Keith finally realized what was missing and what he needed to do to make his peace with God. Here is Keith's story as he tells it:

My story is about miracles.

I attended Sunday school, church, and was even "confirmed" as a child. I believed in God—didn't everybody? I made the mistake of thinking that because I went to church I was automatically a Christian somehow. In reality, I was just going through the motions and my life was filled with anger, bitterness, and resentment. I didn't even know why. At seventeen, I had baseball scouts looking at me for a promising career as a professional baseball player, but a farming accident and the loss of my arm twenty-three years ago changed all that. Instead of thanking God for saving my life, I blamed Him for the loss of my arm. Throughout my life, I maintained a cocky attitude. . . . I was prideful, arrogant, boastful, a know-it-all . . . and full of resentment. I was a successful business owner, yet I was such a miserable, angry human being that nothing in my life was enjoyable, including my marriage.

Everyone around us thought we had the perfect marriage— little did they know. About once a month Lee and I would have the same conversation: she begged and pleaded with me to just be kind. For a day or two I would improve, and then I'd go back to my same mean-spirited ways. At one point I told Lee if I had to choose between my business or her, I would choose my business.

Big surprise there. I was gone most days for ten to twelve hours. I even went to work while she was in the hospital having surgery. I couldn't be inconvenienced! After that, she insisted I see a counselor. I agreed and had one appointment with a secular counselor who said there was nothing wrong with the way I thought or lived my life. That gave me license for my thoughts and actions to be even more and more abusive.

Lee no longer wanted to be in the same room with me, let alone have a relationship with me. Little did I know how God was working to turn my life around—from a life that was so evil into a life that would bring Him glory and praise.

In February I went to a conference where I heard several speakers talk about balance in life. God was revealing to me how messed up my life had become. These speakers actually touched my heart. . . . I actually decided to go home and maybe try this new way of life . . . for a couple of weeks. But God had something different in mind. He started to cleanse me of my pride and arrogance. He took me down to the lowest point in my life, just when I thought my life had a shot at getting better.

Lee no longer believed in me. Our marriage was in crisis. I don't blame her. My wife had had enough of the lies and wanted me out of her life. She was talking divorce; I was contemplating suicide. I got down on my knees, begged for forgiveness, and talked Lee into going to a Christian counselor as a last resort to save our marriage. I was starting to realize I was going to lose my best friend and the love of my life I had hurt and neglected for so many years.

We managed to see a counselor as a couple as well as on an individual basis. I had many more visits because at least this counselor realized that I was really messed up. My last appointment with Lee was the day she told me if things didn't improve in about six months, we should consider divorce.

I didn't want to hear that; I wanted to save my marriage, but all the years of pain and evil had come to a peak. I could do this, I could fix it if God would just give me a little help. But things didn't seem to be getting any better.

During this time, we stumbled into a church where we heard George Kenworthy say that his church was known for saving marriages. Then and there, I knew we were in the right place and that we needed to speak to George as soon as possible. On the day of our appointment, I came home to pick up Lee, but my heart sank when she refused to go.

She snapped, "You broke our marriage, you go fix it!" I turned and went without her. When I arrived, George was not surprised that I came alone. He listened and prayed with me and started to give me biblical truths about God's plan for marriage. I could hardly believe this man—he actually thought he was going to help me save my marriage through God's grace.

Lee agreed to go to the second session in which George asked us his three famous questions: "Do you believe in God? Are you willing to apply biblical principles to your marriage? Are you willing to pray for the Holy Spirit to touch your marriage?" We said yes to all of them. Frankly, I was willing to try anything to save the marriage.

Lee and I continued to go to church, and during the Easter season I discovered what was missing from my life: a real relationship with Jesus. Right then and there I gave my life to Christ. Second Corinthians 5:17 says, "Therefore, if anyone is in Christ, he is a new creation; the old has gone, the new has come!" Once I surrendered my life to God, He made me new from the inside out.

It was then that I finally realized I could do nothing, *nothing* without God. It didn't matter how big my house was; it didn't matter what kind of car I drove; it didn't matter what I did for a living; it didn't matter what club or social circles I belonged to; it didn't matter how much money I had; it didn't matter what kind of clothes I wore; it didn't matter where I went to school or how many degrees I had.

What mattered was that I now had a relationship with the One who could fix the mess I had made of my life and my marriage. Lee and I continued to use the tools George gave us to improve our communication skills, and we prayed for the Holy Spirit to touch and heal our marriage. The things of the world no longer had appeal for us. We began to pray and read devotionals together. I even read Scripture to Lee each night. She said that was the most romantic thing that I had ever done!

On October 12, we met with Pastor George and his co-counselor, Beth Moorhead, in the sanctuary of the church. Standing there in the presence of God, Lee and I exchanged our new vows to each other in the most beautiful ceremony ever. We prayed and recommitted ourselves and our marriage to our Savior. I have never been happier or experienced so much joy in my entire life! So you see, my story is about miracles because God saved my marriage, and He saved me.

Have you, like Keith, invited Jesus into your life? If not, let me encourage you to go for it! Start your marriage makeover right by giving God your life choices. If you aren't sure if you've ever done that, I wish I were sitting in the room with you to lead you in this simple prayer of faith:

> Dear Jesus, I acknowledge I haven't had a heart that loves You. I am sorry for my sins—those actions where I deliberately disobey Your instruction found in the Bible. I am willing to turn from my sins. I openly receive and embrace You as my Savior. I confess You to be the Lord of my life. From this moment on, I want to live for You and serve You. And I ask through the power found in You, that You will begin to work a miracle in my marriage. In Jesus' name, Amen.

Now begins the most exciting time of your life—a season filled with a new strength, a new joy, and a new hope through the power of God's mighty hand!

APPENDICES

THE COMMUNICATION DATE

ELEMENTS OF A SUCCESSFUL COMMUNICATION DATE

I. Feeling of Love

A. Husband shares with his wife the specific ways he felt her love for him over the past week (e.g., rubbed my back, made a pie).

B. Wife shares with her husband the specific ways she felt his love for her over the past week (e.g., washed the dishes, took out the trash).

II. Life Change

A. Husband shares how he has experienced God changing his life over the past week (e.g., through a verse, a prayer, a conversation with someone; or the way he has felt victory over a situation, a mood, or a problem).

B. Husband shares area(s) in his life where God has convicted him of the need to change (e.g., my prayer time is weak; I'm struggling with an attitude toward a person). Rule to remember: You can't identify your spouse as the one with whom you are struggling.

C. Wife shares how she has experienced God changing her life over the past week (e.g., through a verse, a prayer, a conversation with someone) or the ways she has felt victory over a situation, a mood, or a problem.

D. Wife shares area(s) in her life where God has convicted her of the need to change (e.g., my prayer time is weak; I'm struggling with an attitude toward a person). Rule to remember: You can't identify your spouse as the one with whom you are struggling.

III. Pray Together

A. Give thanks to God for the way you have been able to show love toward each other over the past week.

B. Give thanks to God for the way He has changed your lives over the past week.

C. Pray for those areas you've identified that need to change (e.g., attitudes, actions that need to take place).

GUIDELINES FOR THE SUCCESSFUL COMMUNICATION DATE

1. Pick the same time of day and same day of week for your communication date. Guard that time dearly and don't let anything interfere with it!

2. In the course of the communication date, avoid using the pronoun *you* in a negative connotation while referring to your problems (e.g., Pray for me because you're upsetting me.).

3. The communication date should last thirty to thirty-five minutes and go longer only if both parties agree.

4. As the routine of the communication date becomes more familiar, plan on having communication dates more spontaneously and adding more communication dates when you both agree the time is right.

FAMILY BACKGROUND DISCUSSION SHEET

Think about the family in which you grew up. Write down key thoughts about the following areas:

1. How were decisions made? By whom? Who had input and how was it given?

2. How was conflict handled? What happened when your parents did not agree?

3. How were feelings of love, warmth, and tenderness shown?

4. What rituals did your family observe? How were holidays and birthdays celebrated?

5. How were household chores divided? Who did what?

6. How were you disciplined?

7. How were finances handled? What was your part?

8. What was your family's view of recreation? What are three of your happiest memories of family recreation?

9. Describe the temperament of your father, your mother, any siblings, and yourself.

10. How do you think your parents' model has shaped your expectations of what you will be as a helpmate?

11. In what ways have your parents helped each other realize their potential in Christ?

12. What was the spiritual background of your family? What are your beliefs, and how do you express them?

PRAYING SCRIPTURE TO SAVE YOUR MARRIAGE

Here are a number of wonderful passages from the Bible that you might consider using as you pray for God to save or strengthen your marriage. Granted, sometimes the choice of words used in the Bible, though beautiful or poetic, can be difficult to grasp. Since the Bible has been translated in a variety of ways, find a version that's more comfortable to understand. Then use these references to jump-start your prayer time.

Here's how you might turn **Ephesians 6:10–17** (NASB) into a prayer. Personalize it, like this*:

> *I choose to* be strong in the Lord, and in the strength of His might. *I* put on the full armor of God, that *I may* be able to stand firm against the schemes of the devil. For *my* struggle is

**The author's adaptations of the Scripture in this appendix are italicized.*

not against flesh and blood, but against the rulers, against the powers, against the world forces of this darkness, against the spiritual forces of wickedness in the heavenly places.

Therefore, *I* take up the full armor of God, that *I may* be able to resist in the evil day, and having done everything, to stand firm. *I* stand firm therefore, having girded *my* loins with truth, and having put on the breastplate of righteousness, and having shod *my* feet with the preparation of the gospel of peace; in addition to all, *I take* up the shield of faith with which *I* will be able to extinguish all the flaming arrows of the evil one. And *I* take the helmet of salvation, and the sword of the Spirit, which is the word of God.

In **Zechariah 4:6** (NASB) we are reminded that victory comes "not by might nor by power, but by *God's* Spirit." That is what the Lord of hosts says. And that name of God, the Lord of hosts, is a name that He uses often when involved in spiritual warfare. It is a reminder that our God is the Lord of hosts—of incredible numbers of angels who war on our behalf. Ask God to send them into battle on your behalf. He is their commander in chief.

Second Corinthians 10:3–5 (NASB) says,

For though we walk in the flesh, we do not war according to the flesh, for the weapons of our warfare are not of the flesh, but divinely powerful for the destruction of fortresses. We are destroying speculations and every lofty thing raised up against the knowledge of God, and we are taking every thought captive to the obedience of Christ.

Pray **Acts 26:18** (NASB) for your spouse. Pray that his or her eyes will be opened "so that they may turn from darkness to light and from the *control* of Satan" to the arms of a loving God, in order "that they may receive forgiveness of sins and an inheritance among those who have been sanctified by faith" in God.

Read **Daniel 4:34–37** (NASB), and then pray that your spouse, like King Nebuchadnezzar in the passage, will raise his "eyes toward heaven and *his reason will return to him and he will bless the Most High and praise and honor* Him who lives forever." Pray that your spouse will "praise, exalt, and honor the King of heaven, *because* all His works are true and His ways are just, and He is able to humble those who walk in pride."

Pray, according to **John 14:26** (NASB), that "the Helper, the Holy Spirit, whom the Father *has sent in Jesus'* name . . . will teach *your spouse* all things, and bring to *her* remembrance all that *the Lord* has said."

Pray, according to **John 16:8–14** (NASB), that the Holy Spirit "will convict *your spouse* concerning sin and righteousness and judgment." Pray that the Holy Spirit, "the Spirit of truth . . . will guide *your spouse* into all the truth."

Remember, the Lord says in **Jeremiah 32:27** (NASB), "Behold, I am the LORD, the God of all flesh; is anything too difficult for Me?"

Pray, according to **Ephesians 1:17–19** (NASB),

. . . that the God of our Lord Jesus Christ, the Father of glory, may give *to your spouse* a spirit of wisdom and of revelation in the knowledge of Him. *Pray* that the eyes of *his* heart may be enlightened, so that *he may* know what is the hope of His calling, what are the riches of the glory of His inheritance in the saints, and what is the surpassing greatness of His power toward *those* who believe.

And according to **Ephesians 3:14–20** (NASB),

> I bow my knees before the Father, from whom every family in heaven and on earth derives its name, that He would grant *my spouse*, according the riches of His glory, to be strengthened with power through His Spirit in the inner man, so that Christ may dwell in *his heart* through faith; and that *he*, being rooted and grounded in love, may be able to comprehend with all the saints what is the breadth and length and height and depth, and to know the love of Christ which surpasses knowledge, that *he* may be filled up to all fullness of God. *And give the glory* to Him who is able to do far more abundantly beyond all that we ask or think, according to the power that works within us.

Pray **Psalm 57** (NASB) for yourself, especially the first three verses.

> Be gracious to me, O God, be gracious to me, for my soul takes refuge in You; and in the shadow of Your wings I will take refuge, until destruction passes by. I will cry to God Most High, to God who accomplishes all things for me. He will send from heaven and save me; He reproaches him who tramples upon me. God will send forth His lovingkindness and His truth.

Remind yourself of what real love is by reading and praying **1 Corinthians 13** (NASB). Ask the Lord to give you His love for your spouse. Verses 4–8 remind us that

> Love is patient, love is kind and is not jealous; love does not brag and is not arrogant, does not act unbecomingly; it does not seek its own, is not provoked, does not take into account a

wrong suffered, does not rejoice in unrighteousness, but rejoices with the truth; bears all things, believes all things, hopes all things, endures all things. Love never fails.

According to **Jeremiah 31:3** (NASB), ask the Lord to love your spouse "with an everlasting love." Ask Him to draw your spouse with "lovingkindness." If you continue reading in Jeremiah 31, there are some wonderful promises about being rebuilt. According to verses 10 and 11, pray that the Lord will gather your family and keep them "as a shepherd keeps his flock. For the LORD has ransomed *His people* and redeemed *us* from the hand of him who was stronger than *we.*"

In a marital crisis, one or both of you have likely been deceived and caught in Satan's snare. Through prayer in the form of spiritual warfare, we can go after the enemy, with other petitioners, and in the company of God's warrior angels, to rescue the captive. This is similar to the situation that Abraham had with Lot in Genesis 14. Reread that passage from verses 10 to 16 and see how the Lord leads you to pray.

Remember what Joseph said in **Genesis 50:20**. What Satan means for evil, God can use for good. He is sovereign. He will redeem the situation and use it for good.

Read **Romans 8:28–39** (NASB). Remember that "God causes all things to work together for good to those who love God, to those who are called according to His purpose. . . . If God is for us, who *can be* against us?" Jesus is interceding for you! Nothing and no one can separate us from the love of God. "But in all these things we overwhelmingly conquer through Him who loved us."

Remember God's promises in **Jeremiah 29:11–14** (NASB). He says,

"For I know the plans that I have for you," declares the LORD, "plans for welfare and not for calamity to give you a future and a hope. Then you will call upon Me and come and pray to Me, and I will listen to you. And you will seek Me and find Me when you search for Me with all your heart. I will be found by you," declares the LORD, "and I will restore your fortunes and will gather you from all the nations and from all the places where I have driven you," declares the LORD, "and I will bring you back to the place from where I sent you into exile."

When a spouse has moved out and is no longer living with the family, consider them to be in exile. This may also be true when the spouse is emotionally distant from the family.

Psalm 18 (NASB) is full of promises for you. Pray or claim verses 28–40 in particular.

The LORD my God illumines my darkness. For by You I can run upon a troop; and by my God I can leap over a wall. As for God, His way is blameless; the word of the LORD is tried; He is a shield to all who take refuge in Him. For who is God, but the LORD? And who is a rock, except our God, the God who girds me with strength, and makes my way blameless? He makes my feet like hinds' feet (*able to stand firmly or make progress on the dangerous heights of testing and trouble*), and sets me upon my high places. He trains my hands for battle, so that my arms can bend a bow of bronze. You have also given me the shield of Your salvation, and Your right hand upholds me; and Your gentleness makes me great. You enlarge my steps under me, and my feet have not slipped. I pursued my enemies and overtook them, and I did not turn back until they were consumed. I shattered them, so that they were not able to rise; they fell under my feet. For You have girded me with strength for battle;

You have subdued under me those who rose up against me. You have also made my enemies turn their backs to me, and I destroyed those who hated me.

Psalm 37 is full of instruction and promises for you. Pray and claim the entire psalm, as the Lord leads you.

Isaiah 54 and 55 contain many wonderful verses that can be used for prayer. Also look at Isaiah 59–62.

In **Psalm 32:8** (NASB) the Lord says, "I will instruct you and teach you in the way which you should go; I will counsel you with My eye upon you."

Malachi 2:14–16 (AMP) can be prayed in this way:

(Your spouse's name), the Lord was witness [to the covenant made at your marriage] between you and the *husband*/wife of your youth, against whom you have dealt treacherously and to whom you were faithless. Yet *he*/she is your companion and the *husband*/wife of your covenant [made by your marriage vows].

And did not God make [you and your wife/*husband*] one [flesh]? Did not One make you and preserve your spirit alive? And why [did God make you two] one? Because He sought a godly offspring [from your union]. Therefore, take heed to yourselves, and let no one deal treacherously and be faithless to the wife/*husband* of his/*her* youth.

For the Lord, the God of Israel says: "I hate divorce and marital separation, and him *or her* who covers his garment [his wife *or her husband*] with violence. Therefore, keep a watch upon your spirit [that it may be controlled by My Spirit], that you deal not treacherously and faithlessly [with your marriage mate].

Be encouraged by **Joshua 1:9** (NASB) in which the Lord says, "Have I not commanded you? Be strong and courageous! Do not tremble or be dismayed, for the LORD your God is with you wherever you go."

Philippians 1:6 (NASB) reminds us that we can be "confident of this very thing, that He who began a good work in you will perfect it until the day of Christ Jesus."

HELP-ME-HELP-MY-FRIEND GUIDE

Your friend called. His marriage is in trouble—serious trouble—and he needs your help.

Are you ready?

By using this guide and its eight conversation outlines, one for each chapter of the book, you can work alongside your friend, helping him set his marriage back on track.

YOU GOTTA HAVE HOPE

Your friend—the one who is meeting with you because his marriage is in trouble—is likely in desperate need of some hope. Perhaps he's been to counselors, gone to church, studied Scripture, and prayed, and yet feels there is nothing left and nowhere to go. Affirm him for not giving up and for agreeing to meet with you.

CONVERSATION

Ask your friend:

1. WHAT IS YOUR MARITAL SITUATION AT THE PRESENT TIME?
2. WHAT HAVE YOU DONE TO TRY TO IMPROVE IT?
3. HOW ARE YOU FEELING ABOUT YOUR MARRIAGE RIGHT NOW?

Expect to hear the unexpected. If your friend has difficulty expressing his feelings, perhaps you can prime his thinking with some of these

163

common expressions: *troubled, frustrated, worried, trapped, embarrassed, afraid, guilty, exhausted, disappointed, angry, defeated, numb, etc.*

If it hasn't been discussed or made clear already, establish if one or both of the spouses has had or is having an affair. At this time offer no judgment or reaction.

Convey that God is still capable of doing the impossible because of two things:

1. He tells us so in the Bible.

"Behold, I am the LORD, the God of all flesh; is anything too difficult for Me?" (Jeremiah 32:27 NASB). Ask your friend what he sees as the primary impossibilities in his marriage. Be specific. (Don't be surprised if he expresses belief that his overall situation is too difficult for God to restore.)

2. We see evidence.

Tell a personal story of God doing the impossible or read at least one story together from the book. Even when only one spouse is willing to try, it is not an impossible situation for God. Convey that you believe God can do a miracle in his marriage, too.

Review briefly what your friend thinks is the impossible in his marriage. Remind him that what he can't do, God can. Going through your friend's list of impossibilities, affirm out loud that God can ___, God can ___, and God can ___.

Express the following: God loves you profoundly. He cares about you personally. He cares about your marriage and about your family. He makes his abundant resources—riches, strength, power, and might— available to you. Give God one more chance.

Ask your friend the three main questions presented in the book:

1. DO YOU BELIEVE THAT THERE IS A GOD?
2. ARE YOU WILLING TO APPLY THE PRINCIPLES OF THE BIBLE TO YOUR LIFE?
3. WILL YOU PRAY FOR GOD TO STRENGTHEN YOU AND YOUR SPOUSE?

If any of the answers are no, relay another story of a changed marriage if it seems appropriate.

ASSIGNMENTS

For You

1. MAKE "THE ONE THING" 3" X 5" CARD WITH JEREMIAH 32:27 FOR YOUR FRIEND TO TAKE HOME.
2. CALL YOUR FRIEND AT LEAST ONCE THIS WEEK TO ENCOURAGE HIM.
3. PRAY SOME OF THE SUGGESTED SCRIPTURES FOR HIS MARRIAGE. (SEE APPENDIX C.)
4. CONTINUE READING *Before the Last Resort.*
5. LOOK AHEAD TO CHAPTER 2 AND PREPARE THE "THE ONE THING" ASSIGNMENT.

For Your Friend

1. AVOID ALL NEGATIVE TALK; BAD-MOUTHING ONLY INCREASES YOUR PAIN AND DISCOURAGEMENT.
2. USE YOUR JEREMIAH 32:27 CARD FREQUENTLY. MAKE MORE THAN ONE AND PLACE THEM AROUND THE HOUSE, CAR, ETC. IF YOU NEED TO REMIND YOURSELF MORE OFTEN THAT GOD CAN!
3. PRAY SCRIPTURE FOR YOUR MARRIAGE. (SEE APPENDIX C.)
4. BEGIN READING *Before the Last Resort.*

WHEN PRAYER DOESN'T WORK

When we're in deep pain, hearing something like "The answer is in the Bible" might seem trite. Illustration: In second-year algebra the answers to the odd problems are usually in the back of the textbook. They are there to help the student see if his work has led him to the correct response. The student, however, cannot just copy the answers; he must show the work that led to the right solution. Likewise, knowing biblical truth does not always lift our spirits immediately. God's answers are still the right answers, but often we must go through challenging steps that lead us to fully rely on Him.

CONVERSATION

Ask your friend:

1. HAVE YOU BEEN AVOIDING NEGATIVE TALK?
2. IN WHAT WAYS HAVE YOUR RECENT DAYS BEEN BETTER OR WORSE?

Share the following about faith: Believing God's answers are the right ones, even when we don't see it or feel it, is called faith. Here is what the prophet Habakkuk said when facing significant troubles:

> Though the fig tree should not blossom
> And there be no fruit on the vines,
> Though the yield of the olive should fail
> And the fields produce no food,
> Though the flock should be cut off from the fold
> And there be no cattle in the stalls,
> Yet I will exult in the LORD,
> I will rejoice in the God of my salvation.
> The Lord God is my strength.
>
> HABAKKUK 3:17–19 (NASB)

Discuss:

1. HOW BIG WAS HABAKKUK'S VIEW OF GOD?
2. DO YOU HAVE A SIMILAR VIEW OF GOD? IF NOT, DESCRIBE YOUR VIEW OF GOD.
3. WHAT MIGHT CAUSE US TO UNDERESTIMATE THE GREATNESS OF GOD?
4. DO YOU UNDERSTAND HOW YOUR VIEW OF GOD IS CRITICAL TO BELIEVING THAT HE HAS THE ABILITY TO RESTORE YOUR MARRIAGE?

Together, rewrite a version of the Habakkuk passage using a format such as this:

Though _____ and _____,
though _____ and _____,
I will rejoice in the God of my salvation.
The Lord God is my strength.

Everything you write in the blanks is within the realm of what God can do. Remember your index card: "Behold, I am the LORD, the God of all flesh; is anything too difficult for me?" (Jeremiah 32:27 NASB).

Read this adaptation of a benediction Paul wrote in Ephesians 3:20–21. Write it out for your friend to take home. This is "The One Thing" assignment.

Now to him who is able

Now to him who is able to do immeasurably

Now to him who is able to do immeasurably more

Now to him who is able to do immeasurably more than all
    we ask

Now to him who is able to do immeasurably more than all
    we ask or imagine,

Now to him who is able to do immeasurably more than all
    we ask or imagine, according to his power that is at work
    within us,

To him be glory . . . Amen.

ASSIGNMENT

For You

1. CALL YOUR FRIEND AT LEAST ONCE THIS WEEK.

2. CONTINUE PRAYING SCRIPTURE FOR HIS MARRIAGE.

3. CONTINUE READING *Before the Last Resort*.

4. LOOK AHEAD TO CHAPTER 3 AND PREPARE A "STOP. THINK." CARD FOR YOUR FRIEND.

For Your Friend

1. CONTINUE AVOIDING NEGATIVE TALK.

2. CONTINUE READING *Before the Last Resort.* BE SURE TO INCLUDE CHAPTER 2 IF POSSIBLE.

3. POST THE EPHESIANS 3 BENEDICTION WHERE YOU WILL SEE IT FREQUENTLY.

ATTITUDE IS EVERYTHING

Pray with your friend.

Ask how the past several days have been. Even if his responses are negative, reassure him that God makes power available to help change the pattern of negative thinking. Explain that attitude plays a key role in overcoming difficulties.

CONVERSATION

Ask your friend which of the following thought patterns have been part of his recent mind-set. Continue with a discussion of each, using the provided thoughts as a starting point.

- HOPELESSNESS
- MISPERCEPTION OF GOD
- SELF-PITY

- BLAMING OTHERS

Hopelessness: Review some of what you discussed in the first session. If your friend seems to be stuck in hopelessness, perhaps he needs to consider grief counseling. Hopelessness must be overcome.

Misperception of God: You should have already discussed what it means to underestimate the greatness of God. There are other ways we can be mistaken in our thinking about God. A common misperception is one of extremes: either God is too lenient or too harsh.

If we view Him as being too lenient, we might conclude that God would not want us unhappy, so we begin to rationalize poor choices. The limitation of this view is that we reduce God to something less than He is, and we fail to grasp the hope, riches, and power that He has for us. On the other hand, if we view Him too harshly we focus on his justice, as a God who demands performance from us. We feel that God wants to zap us because we are struggling, so we feel completely defeated and unloved. The limitation of this view is that we aren't recognizing God's mercy and desire to bring us to right relationship and healing.

Self-pity: This causes us to stay in our misery much longer than we need to. Because we are so focused on ourselves, we wrongly presume upon the motives and actions of others toward us. We can, in fact, become angry when we feel that others are not as concerned about us as we think they should be. We can also easily become jealous of those who may not seem to have any problems. Self-pity makes our situation the center of the universe.

Blaming Others: It is so easy to blame others for our pain. However, our constant joy is dependent on our relationship with Jesus, not on how we are treated by those around us. While this is challenging to do when your marriage is falling apart, you need to come to the place of understanding that real joy and peace do not come from your spouse's behavior.

Explain the "Stop. Think." card process.

ASSIGNMENT

For You

1. CALL AND ENCOURAGE YOUR FRIEND AT LEAST ONCE THIS WEEK.
2. BE PREPARED TO EXPLAIN THE COMMUNICATION DATE NEXT WEEK. (SEE APPENDIX A.)

For Your Friend

1. CONTINUE TO PRAY SCRIPTURE FOR YOUR MARRIAGE.
2. USE THE "STOP. THINK." CARD AS OFTEN AS NEEDED THIS WEEK.

LOOK WHO'S TALKING

Pray with your friend.

Ask your friend how he has been working to adjust his thinking in order to have a right attitude.

CONVERSATION

Explain to your friend that even though he may feel that his spouse is being adversarial, perhaps she is simply experiencing communication breakdowns that can be overcome. Ask him to rank, on a scale of 1 to 5, how he is communicating in conversations with his spouse.

Every conversation is a heated argument		We can't talk much without disagreeing		We have great talks and listen well to each other
1	2	3	4	5

Discuss: Do you believe the average listener only hears about 20 percent of a conversation? Do you realize that when you speak, not one but six messages can be heard? Think of a recent conversation. Which of the following messages do you think was conveyed?

- WHAT YOU MEANT TO SAY
- WHAT YOU ACTUALLY SAID
- WHAT THE OTHER PERSON HEARD
- WHAT THE OTHER PERSON THOUGHT THEY HEARD
- WHAT THE OTHER PERSON SAID ABOUT WHAT YOU SAID
- WHAT YOU THOUGHT THE OTHER PERSON SAID ABOUT WHAT YOU SAID[19]

Proverbs contains many wise sayings about the way we communicate. What problem does the following verse address?

> He who gives an answer before he hears, it is folly and shame to him.
>
> 18:13 (NASB)

Do you ever—or often—speak without listening? Or is listening what you do while waiting for your next opportunity to speak? Discuss how doing so might affect the outcome of one of your conversations (perhaps even a conversation you need to have with your spouse).

Another verse from Proverbs says,

> He who guards his mouth and his tongue, guards his soul from troubles.
>
> 21:23 (NASB)

Do you ever blurt things out and then wish you hadn't said them? Thinking first is always a wise choice. Besides avoiding saying what we later regret, it helps us say what we truly desire to say and makes what we say more acceptable because we haven't invalidated it with folly.

Have your friend try to identify an insensitive comment he's blurted out recently and how it demonstrated a lack of forethought. Help him make the connection between how he converses with his spouse and how that contributes to conflict.

Learning when to speak and what to say are nonoptional skills for winning in marriage. Because we often communicate love with our words, applying the principles of good communication is critically important. However, even when we learn to communicate well with our words, we might not be expressing love to our spouse. This is due to the fact that words are not everyone's "love language." The chapter goes into more detail about this. Review that material now if you feel that it would be helpful.

ASSIGNMENT

For You

1. CALL AND ENCOURAGE YOUR FRIEND AT LEAST ONCE THIS WEEK.
2. PREPARE "THE ONE THING" ASSIGNMENT FOR CHAPTER 5, WRITING THE SIX RULES FOR A GOOD, CLEAN FIGHT ON A SHEET OF PAPER FOR YOUR FRIEND.

For Your Friend

1. GO ON A COMMUNICATION DATE WITH YOUR SPOUSE.
2. CONTINUE USING THE "STOP. THINK." CARD OR OTHER ATTITUDE ADJUSTMENT REMINDERS.
3. CONTINUE REFERRING TO JEREMIAH 32:27 FOR A REMINDER THAT "GOD CAN!"
4. PRAY FOR YOUR SPEECH TO BE HUMBLE, HONEST, AND HELPFUL.

HAVE YOURSELF A GOOD, CLEAN FIGHT

Pray with your friend. Encourage him to pray also.

Ask: Did you go on a communication date with your spouse? How did it go? Did you apply listening and thinking before speaking (either on your date or in another setting)?

CONVERSATION

In this life it is not possible to avoid conflict completely. God knows this is the case and He gives us some guidance about how to handle conflict. From the Bible, read Ephesians 4:25–32 aloud together.

The way we handle conflict might have something to do with patterns we learned from our parents. Did they have yelling matches? Did they retreat to opposite corners of the house? Or did they each come out with their feelings in a civilized manner? Each of these approaches is labeled respectively: the shouters, the pouters, and the outers. Ask your friend to determine the style he observed most in childhood and the style that he personally practices most.

Talk through the rules for fighting that were presented in the chapter:

Rule 1: **Remember, you are on the same team.** Couples waste time trying to prove whose version of previous events is the right one. This only lengthens the argument and widens the division.

Rule 2: **Check your weapons to make sure they are not deadly.** We all know words can be used as weapons, even truthful words. What makes the difference between fair words and fatal words?

Rule 3: **Agree together that the time is right.** There is a right time and wrong time to work through a conflict. In any marriage one partner might always think they are ready to deal with it, while the other never seems ready. Identify some of the right and wrong times.

Rule 4: **Remember that the aim of the fight should be edification.** Ephesians 4:29 says that our words can give grace to the hearer. What does that mean? What are some words and phrases that would give grace during difficult discussions?

Rule 5: **Work out your conflict with your spouse, not your friends.** How is sharing your struggles with too many people detrimental to healing your marriage? If you have been careless about this, will you commit to limit the circle to only those who need to know?

Rule 6: Heed the prompting of God when He nudges you to seek forgiveness and oneness. Because we are now expecting God to heal your marriage, we should ask God to make you more sensitive to know and understand when He is speaking in your mind. He can help you remember the Bible verses you've read and other changes you've begun making over the past several weeks.

Ask: What is the most important rule for you from today's session? Why?

ASSIGNMENT

For You

1. CALL YOUR FRIEND TO UPLIFT HIM AT LEAST ONCE THIS WEEK.

2. REREAD CHAPTER 6 FOR NEXT TIME AND BE ESPECIALLY FAMILIAR WITH THE APPLICABLE MALE/FEMALE SECTION.

For Your Friend

1. PLACE YOUR RULES FOR CONFLICT SOMEWHERE PROMINENT (FOR EXAMPLE, YOUR BATHROOM MIRROR). TRY TO PUT THEM INTO PRACTICE THIS WEEK.

2. CONTINUE TO USE THE "STOP. THINK." CARD OR OTHER ATTITUDE ADJUSTMENT METHOD.

3. PRAY FOR YOUR MARRIAGE.

BLUEPRINT FOR A MARRIAGE MAKEOVER

Pray with your friend.

Ask: How have you seen God work in you or your marriage lately? How have you used the rules for clean, fair fighting? Are they making a difference?

CONVERSATION

Discuss: Where have you typically gone for marriage guidance—parents, advice books or columns, friends? Have they been helpful for long-term problems—why or why not?

This session deals with how God can help you handle problems and restore your marriage. Let's look at some Bible verses that describe the kind of thoughts and actions a husband and wife can put in place in order to work toward restoration.

For the Husband

> Likewise, husbands, live with your wives in an understanding way, showing honor to the woman as the weaker vessel, since they are heirs with you of the grace of life, so that your prayers may not be hindered.
>
> 1 PETER 3:7 (ESV)

Two essential building blocks for men can be found in this verse: (1) the building block of understanding, and (2) the building block of honor. Look back in the chapter and discuss what each of these building blocks does for a marriage.

Ask: Can you think of a time when you did something for your wife that you thought she would appreciate but didn't? Was it something you would have really liked if she had done it for you? Is it possible that it didn't meet her need?

There are five ways listed where men tend not to fully understand their wives.

1. WE DON'T UNDERSTAND THEIR LOVE NEEDS.
2. WE DON'T UNDERSTAND HOW THEY THINK.
3. WE DON'T UNDERSTAND HOW TO BE A HELP TO THEM.
4. WE DON'T UNDERSTAND THEIR EMOTIONS.
5. WE DON'T UNDERSTAND THEIR NEED FOR RELATIONSHIP.[20]

Ask your friend to choose one of these where he will intentionally work to understand his wife better.

For the Wife

> Likewise, wives, be subject to your own husbands, so that even
> if some do not obey the word, they may be won without a word
> by the conduct of their wives—when they see your respectful
> and pure conduct. Do not let your adorning be external—
> the braiding of hair, the wearing of gold, or the putting on
> of clothing—but let your adorning be the hidden person of
> the heart with the imperishable beauty of a gentle and quiet
> spirit, which in God's sight is very precious. For this is how the
> holy women who hoped in God used to adorn themselves, by
> submitting to their husbands, as Sarah obeyed Abraham calling
> him lord. And you are her children if you do good and do not
> fear anything that is frightening.
>
> 1 PETER 3:1–6 (ESV)

Wives are given three essential building blocks: (1) action, (2) adornment, and (3) attitude. Look back in the chapter and discuss what each of these building blocks does for a marriage.

Ask: What would it look like if you were to completely trust God to change your husband? How might you need to change your attitude or behavior?

ASSIGNMENT

For You

1. CONTINUE PRAYING FOR GOD TO HEAL YOUR FRIEND'S MARRIAGE.
2. IF POSSIBLE, PREPARE A ROMANCE GIFT PACKAGE FOR YOUR FRIEND. SEE THE END OF CHAPTER 7 FOR TWO RESOURCE IDEAS AND/OR COME UP WITH ADDITIONAL IDEAS OF YOUR OWN.

For Your Friend

1. FOCUS ON THE APPLICABLE MALE OR FEMALE SECTION OF CHAPTER 6 IN *Before the Last Resort.*

2. CONSIDER WHICH BUILDING BLOCK YOU WILL BEGIN TO BETTER UTILIZE IN YOUR MARRIAGE AND ASK GOD TO HELP YOU DO SO.

GUIDE 7

ROMANCE BY THE BOOK

Pray with your friend. Invite him to pray also.

Ask: How have you been using the marriage building blocks (for example, understanding, honor, action, adornment, or attitude) in your relationship with your spouse? What results are you experiencing in your life and in the relationship?

CONVERSATION

Discuss: Perhaps you and your spouse have not experienced romance for quite some time. Is it difficult for you to believe that a healthy sexual relationship is possible? You might have to reintroduce romance into your relationship at a defined pace. How are you feeling about intimacy with your mate right now?

Romance is sometimes challenging even in healthy marriages. Add conflict to the mix, or something as threatening as an affair, and romance disappears quickly. What barriers to intimacy are you and your spouse encountering?

If your friend or his spouse has been involved in an affair, talk through this section carefully.

Affairs are probably the greatest threat to marriage, and most certainly are to physical intimacy within marriage. Understanding how an affair often develops can help in rebuilding what has been destroyed. The typical progression leading to an affair is:

1. WE FEEL THAT OUR NEEDS ARE NOT BEING MET, SO WE CONCLUDE THAT OUR SPOUSE DOES NOT LOVE US.

2. WE BUILD UP WALLS TO PROTECT OURSELVES FROM THE PAIN OF UNFULFILLED NEEDS AND EVENTUALLY CONCLUDE THAT WE DO NOT LOVE OUR SPOUSE.

3. WHEN WE CONCLUDE THAT WE DO NOT LOVE OUR SPOUSE AND THAT OUR SPOUSE DOES NOT REALLY LOVE US, WE BEGIN TO WONDER IF WE WERE OUT OF THE WILL OF GOD WHEN WE GOT MARRIED OR IF GOD WOULD WANT US TO STAY IN A SITUATION THAT IS MAKING US UNHAPPY.

4. SOMEONE COMES ALONG WHO MEETS OUR NEEDS. AFTER A WHILE, WE CONCLUDE THAT WE LOVE THE ONE WHO IS MEETING OUR NEEDS.

Ask: Can you identify with any of the steps in this progression? If so, explain.

If your friend has had an affair and has not dealt with it biblically, ask: *What do you think Jesus wants you to do?* (This is an appropriate question. Do not hesitate to make it clear that adultery is sin.) Voice confidence that God will give him strength to end the affair if he hasn't done so already.

If your friend's spouse had an affair, ask: *Are you willing to forgive and to work together at rebuilding trust and intimacy?* Encourage him that God has power to heal his marriage and to restore genuine love.

The Song of Solomon in the Bible is a beautiful love play presented through poetry. Chapter 7 explains the play. From what we learn about how Solomon and his bride communicated their love to one another, try one of these exercises:

- WRITE A SENTENCE OR TWO PRAISING YOUR SPOUSE FOR TWO OR MORE QUALITIES YOU ADMIRE ABOUT HER PHYSICALLY, EMOTIONALLY, SPIRITUALLY, AND/OR INTELLECTUALLY.

- THINK OF A WAY THAT YOU CAN NONVERBALLY DEMONSTRATE TO YOUR SPOUSE THAT SHE IS YOUR TOP PRIORITY.

ASSIGNMENT

For You

1. GIVE YOUR FRIEND THE ROMANCE PACKAGE YOU HAVE PREPARED. ENCOURAGE HIM TO BEGIN THE ROAD BACK TO INTIMACY WITH HIS SPOUSE.

2. PRAY FOR HIM TO PICTURE WHAT THEIR RELATIONSHIP WOULD BE LIKE IF GOD WERE TO GENUINELY RESTORE THEIR MARRIAGE.

For Your Friend

1. READ THE SONG OF SOLOMON IN THE BIBLE.

2. FOLLOW THROUGH ON THE SONG OF SOLOMON APPLICATION.

3. HUG YOUR SPOUSE IF SHE WILL RECEIVE IT.

SEEING IS BELIEVING

Pray together with your friend.

Ask: How are you seeing God at work in your life? In your marriage? What have you done to nonverbally communicate love to your spouse?

CONVERSATION

Use this time to review your previous sessions, asking: What is the key thought or commitment you've made from each of the previous seven chapters regarding

- HOPE?
- FAITH?
- YOUR ATTITUDE?
- COMMUNICATION?

- FIGHTING FAIR?
- REBUILDING YOUR MARRIAGE?
- ROMANCE?

ASSIGNMENT

For You

1. CONTINUE PRAYING SCRIPTURE FOR YOUR FRIEND'S MARRIAGE.
2. CONTINUE CALLING YOUR FRIEND WEEKLY TO ENCOURAGE HIM.

For Your Friend

1. FINISH READING *Before the Last Resort.*
2. CONTINUE WITH ALL APPLICATIONS AND COMMITMENTS.
3. CONTINUE TO PRAY SCRIPTURE FOR YOUR MARRIAGE.

ACKNOWLEDGMENTS

I am deeply grateful for all the friends and family who encouraged me to write this book. First, thanks to my wife, Joan, who has challenged me for many years to put in print this record of what we have seen God do in the lives of many people. Thanks to my wonderful congregation at the Wayzata Evangelical Free Church who not only listened to the sermons that formed the basis of this work but also gave me valuable feedback. Thanks to my good friend Paul Ridgeway. Paul, you prayed for me, supported me, and worked harder than a friend should have to, to make this book a reality.

In addition, I am indebted to the "brave hearts" whose stories are in this book. Your courage in allowing me to publish your marriage makeovers is an inspiration to me and a credit to the Lord Jesus.

I could not have written this book without the help of all my counseling partners. Thankfully, early in my ministry, God showed me how desperately I needed the woman's perspective to help couples, so he brought me an army of compassionate, godly women who have been willing to sit at my side and help families in crisis. I am especially grateful for Mary Sue Ong, who assisted me in raising up counselors in Colorado; Marti Lambrides, who did the same in Indiana; and Beth Moorhead, who has been my right arm in Minnesota. Thanks, ladies, for your commitment to Jesus and all the long, fatiguing hours you invested to equip the church to meet the needs of couples in conflict!

I am a preacher and I know that writing a book is very different from preparing a sermon. I could not have done this project without the help of my son. George, you have been an extraordinary editor and you have motivated me to stay the course. Thanks, too, to all who read the manuscript and gave input: Cindy Hamilton, Jan Hamilton, Ling Yang, and Rick Gallagher. Special thanks to Bob DeMoss. Bob, your suggestions have been insightful and your editing gave clarity and vitality to the ideas in this book.

Finally, I am grateful to my new friends at FamilyLife who have given me the opportunity to tell my story. Margie Clark, you have been my champion. Thanks for your enthusiastic support and for leading the charge in completing all the little things that it takes to publish a book.

Thanks to the Lord Jesus. This book is really Your story about what You can do in the lives of those who dare to believe in You. May this book bring glory to Your name!

NOTES

1. Unless otherwise noted in the text, the names of all couples and the cities used throughout this book have been changed to protect privacy.

2. Tim LaHaye, *How to Win Over Depression* (Grand Rapids: Zondervan, 1974), 117.

3. Ibid.

4. Helen H. Lemmel, "Turn Your Eyes Upon Jesus" Baptist Hymnal, 1975 ed. (Nashville: Convention Press, 1975), 198.

5. "Doxology," Words by Thomas Ken, 1695. Public Domain.

6. Norman Wright gave a training session for the Taylor Johnson Temperament Analysis test in Cedar Rapids, Iowa, in 1984, and introduced this technique.

7. Dale Carnegie, *How to Stop Worrying and Start Living* (New York: Pocket Books, 1984), 99.

8. Norman Wright, *Communication: Key to Your Marriage* (Ventura: Regal Books, 1974), 54.

9. For more on this see Chuck Swindoll, *Strike the Original Match* (Carol Stream: Tyndale), 127-146. See also, Charlie Shedd, *Letters to Karen*, 206.

10. D. Keith Mano, "Sin" *People Magazine*, May 23, 1986.

11. "The 10 Most Expensive Celebrity Divorces," Forbes.com, April 12, 2007, http://www.forbes.com/2007/04/12/most-expensive-divorces -biz-cz_lg_0412celebdivorce.html.

12. Ibid.

13. Ibid.

14. Ibid.

15. Jean Cummings, *Movie Star Magazine* (June 2001). http://www.johnnydeppfan.com/interviews/msjune2001.htm.

16. Gary Chapman, *The Five Love Languages* (Chicago: Northfield Publishing, 2004), 10.

17. John Gray, *Men Are from Mars, Women Are from Venus* (New York: HarperCollins, 1992), 31.

18. Jim Davidson, "Seven Stages of a Marriage Cold," *The Courier-Post*, April 17, 1999.

19. Norman Wright

20. Ibid.

Get the Most out of
The Smart Stepfamily!

For more resources and insight from Ron Deal, visit smartstepfamilies.com.

These eight sessions support *The Smart Stepfamily* book and are ideal for small groups, seminars, or individual couples. Ron Deal's personable presentation combines instruction and encouragement, offering useable solutions and tips for everyday living.

The Smart Stepfamily DVD

This interactive workbook is guaranteed to help you get the most out of *The Smart Stepfamily*. It includes discussion questions for before and after each DVD session, space to take notes, bonus reading material, leader instructions, and guidelines for facilitating effective groups.

The Smart Stepfamily Participant's Guide

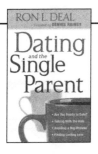

More Resources From Ron Deal
When children are involved, dating gets complicated. In this book, Ron Deal guides single parents—and those who date them—through the emotional ups and downs of dating with kids, including how to navigate relationships, avoid potential pitfalls, and strengthen their families.

Dating and the Single Parent

TO ORDER, VISIT SHOP.FAMILYLIFE.COM
OR CALL 1-800-FL-TODAY